MIRACLES OF HEALING FOR YOU TODAY!

by
Oral Roberts

A prescription toward your total health from the man who has personally touched and prayed for more than a million sick people and believed God with them for their healing and health.

MIRACLES OF HEALING FOR YOU TODAY

by

Oral Roberts

Unless otherwise indicated,
all Scripture quotations are from
the King James Version of the
Bible.

TABLE OF CONTENTS

CHAPTER   **PAGE**

1   Do you need healing? I can help you. But I can't do it unless you let me. 9

2   You are sick in some way. Jesus has given me something to say to you *now*. This is *your* moment to hear it. 13

3   You must have a *SOURCE* for *your* healing. 20

4   The way God works is based on the seed. You must do things the way God does them. Here's how. 25

5   You *must* quit dividing the natural and the supernatural. 34

6   You must quit blaming God for the way things are in your life today. 42

7   You've got to TAKE CHARGE of your attitude. 50

8   You've got to trade in your poor attitudes for some better ones. 58

9   Here's how I took charge of my attitude to correct the worst mistake of my life. And if I could do it in the shape I was in, YOU can do it today! 66

10   A change in *your* attitude CAN and WILL change circumstances around you. 78

11   I can hardly wait until your health BURSTS FORTH! You've got to grab hold of that moment. Here's how. 90

12 A burst of healing is something you can KEEP or LOSE. You've got to KEEP it! 100

13 You've got to use a POINT OF CONTACT to move into greater and GREATER health! 109

14 You must get your attitude into YOUR hand and turn it into a POINT OF CONTACT. 115

15 You've got to use the *Name of Jesus*. He's the most powerful tool you have. 126

16 You've got to settle the matter of death once and for all. 137

17 You've got to take action EACH TIME a crisis hits. 144

18 You've got to get your eyes on the FINAL GOAL of the health Jesus has for YOU!. 155

19 Let's pull it all together now. 162

20 I tell you again...I can help you more than this book—but you have to let me. 167

CITY OF FAITH
Medical and Research Center

I believe Oral Roberts is called by God to be a healing evangelist: to preach, teach and heal. The same God he serves called me just as clearly to be a physician and surgeon.

When Oral felt led of God to ask me to help him build the City of Faith Medical and Research Center, I felt God leading me to accept and give my best. We have spent thousands of hours together in the Word of God, in prayer, in frank discussion, in seeking God as the Source of all healing, and in trying to fulfill the calling: "Take My healing power to your generation."

This book in your hand is the most exciting, indeed the frankest, I've ever read on healing. It's more than a book; it's a way of life that leads you to change your life and to have better health in every area of your life.

Oral has 35 years — over a third of a century — in dealing face-to-face with over a million sick people. And with millions more through his television programs and letters.

He is going to come right at you. Get ready to take action. He is a man who cares for you, hurts for you, and is committed like no other man I know to obey God to help you, no matter what it takes.

Oral Roberts helps me as a man, a husband and father, a doctor, a Christian. . . and he's going to help you. Let it HAPPEN to you.

James E Winslow Jr. M.D.

Dr. James E. Winslow, Jr.
Orthopedic Surgeon and Chief Executive Officer
City of Faith Medical and Research Center

Dr. Jim Winslow — my faithful partner and colaborer in helping to build God's City of Faith.

①

Do you need healing?
I can help you.
But I can't do it
Unless you let me.

"Oral Roberts, I need help."

I took one look at the man sitting across from me, and I could tell immediately that his situation was desperate. It was obvious. His health was gone. Deep lines of pain were etched into his white face. I suspected that his finances had been draining away for months and the strain upon his family was severe.

"I need help so bad, Oral Roberts, that I don't know what to do or where to turn. I thought maybe you'd know what to do."

I said, "I *do* know many things to do. God has told me how I can help you. But I can't do it unless you let me."

"Well, I sure will let you."

9

"Don't be too quick to answer," I said. "It's going to take 100 percent cooperation from both of us."

"I will cooperate. I *must* have help."

"And you have to start by letting the faith you have – even if it's just a little – go out of your heart up to God."

"I will. Oh, I will."

I could sense the urgency in his voice…see just a glimmer of hope…the beginning of expecting a miracle that things would change. And I said, "Then I know that I know that *we* – together with God – can get *your* health moving in the right direction. You can get on the road to the total health God has designed and prescribed for you."

We agreed together, and we started to work.

Now, friend…

God has told me in plain language that I can help *you*…*you* holding this book…*you* reading these words. I can help you get through this year and through the crises that hit your life all the way through it. He has given me the discernment and the authority to help you get into better health and prosperity, as they come from Him. I ask God to drive into your spirit the clear understanding that *no matter what* sickness or disharmony you experience in your body and spirit…*God did not plant it*…God does not want it…and God is absolutely determined to bring you into greater health and wholeness.

You say, "If you could do that, I would cooperate with you 100 percent."

And I say back to you, if *you* will start on that basis and let just a little of *your* faith go out of your heart up to God – I know that I know that I know that *with God*, we can get YOUR health moving in the right direction. *You* too can get on the road to the TOTAL health God has designed and prescribed for *you*.

If you will do what I tell you to do in this little book, I will go to sleep tonight knowing deep inside me that some of the best help – spiritually, physically, financially, emotionally, and in relationships with your dear loved ones – will START almost IMMEDIATELY in your favor, and in the days ahead you can come to have a new lease on life.

I believe it. I feel it. I know it. I can see it coming.

But let me alert you on an emergency basis – just as I would if a cyclone were coming your way and I could see that it would wipe you out if you didn't get out of there in a hurry.

The alert is this: there is something *you* have to do. You're going to have to deal God personally into your life. God fixed it so you *can* do it…and ONLY you can choose to do it. You're going to have *to choose to take charge of your attitude*. You're going to have to choose to take action. You…you…you…are going to have to choose.

Now hear me. You *can* do it. And I'm going to help you. I'm going to show you how in the pages ahead. There are three people involved right now in your getting well – Jesus, you, and Oral Roberts. And together, we can get you into better health than you've ever dreamed about.

MY MOTHER ASKED ME THESE QUESTIONS AND NOW I ASK YOU...

Are you listening?

Do you have a listening heart?

Are you listening? That means really *hearing*. I want you to block everything else out of your mind. Get up and close the door if you need to. Shut out what's happening around you. Maybe you need to wait until the rest of your family is in bed to read this book. I want you to PAY AT-TENTION and listen closely to what I have to say. I want your undivided attention. It can make the difference between sickness and health. Are you listening?

Do you have a listening heart? Now that's different than just listening. To have a listening heart means that

11

you have opened yourself up to bold new ideas that God may want to plant in your life. Are you willing to begin to learn something new...to choose to make some changes in your attitude – and I do mean YOUR personal attitude – that is totally in line with the Bible and the teachings of Jesus?

IF you aren't willing to start right now to LEARN to listen and to make up your mind to develop a listening heart...there's not much I can do for you, friend. You might as well close this book and go on about your business of being sick and getting sicker...or of being down and getting *downer*.

As the old saying goes:

> *Without God, I cannot;*
> *But without me, God will not.*

Are you listening?

Do you have a listening heart?

If you are willing to try...then I've got life-changing news for you. And I'm so eager to share it, I can hardly write the next words to you fast enough...

You are sick in some way. Jesus has given me something to say to you now. This is your moment to hear it.

Back in the early days of my healing ministry, I'd sometimes turn to a crowd – or say on the radio or in a letter:

"IF YOU WILL DO WHAT I TELL YOU TO
DO, A MIRACLE WILL START HAPPENING
IN YOUR LIFE."

Folks in the late 1940's weren't accustomed to a preacher being so anointed of God, so caring for their healing, and so burning with desire to preach God's deliverance in order that people could get *whole* again. They weren't accustomed to a preacher who spoke with authority, and who was so anointed with the Holy Spirit burning in his soul that he couldn't stand still until he

13

poured out everything he was expressing that very moment to them.

I admit I was – and am – a different breed. I haven't always been, though. I had settled down into that regular Sunday morning church routine like a lot of other preachers – a song by the choir, announcements, lead in prayer, take up an offering, preach, close with prayer, go home. But God had moved in on me, and He wouldn't let me alone. He told me to start speaking and preaching and teaching and praying for people to get WELL...and to actually take His healing power around the world and in definite ways to MY generation.

I had to OBEY. He told me to tell the people:

"IF YOU WILL DO WHAT I TELL YOU TO DO, A MIRACLE WILL START HAPPENING IN YOUR LIFE."

Two months after I started the healing ministry in 1947, a specific incident happened that I can see right now as clearly as if it had happened yesterday. I had finished a message about Jesus coming to save us and heal us IN THE NOW. I had already begun to pray for the sick people who were at the meeting.

I came to a woman who had been carried to the meeting in a kitchen chair. She had been carried around in that chair for eight years because she had severe arthritis. Her body was all knotted up. Just one look told me she was really suffering.

As I came toward this woman that night, I saw a flicker of light in her eyes and on her face. I could feel deep inside me that this woman was near to walking into her miracle. She was beginning to believe that God didn't want her to be carried around on a kitchen chair all bound up with arthritis. She had heard a Bible-packed, anointed sermon and she had let it sink into her attitude. She was getting an attitude of believing that a man named Oral

Roberts had been sent to pray for her that she might be free again.

(On my part, I was discerning by the Holy Spirit that I was to give her a definite word from the Lord, even though she was only one among the audience.)

She was near to being *ready* in her attitude for God to work in her life. But she wasn't accustomed to somebody talking straight to her like I was about to do. I looked her right in the eye and said:

> "Sister, the Lord is telling me in my heart that
> I am to tell you to do something."

She just looked at me.

I said, "If you will do what I tell you to do, I believe your healing will *begin* in a matter of seconds."

She stared at me.

I said again, "If you will do what I tell you to do, I believe your healing can begin in a matter of seconds."

She nodded her head, but she still didn't know what I meant.

I could feel something begin to stir in the crowd. I sensed that people weren't used to a man of God talking like that.

And then I said to her, "In the Name of JESUS, be healed. START getting up out of that chair and take your first step."

Someone later told me that my voice rang out like a shot, penetrating the entire building. Others told me they felt like my voice had gotten inside of them and they were hearing from the Lord that they were to get up and start being healed.

At that moment, I was in tune with Jesus as much as I've ever been. I felt Him, and I continue to feel Him. I'm a JESUS man...a man who Jesus lives in, moves in, and acts through.

For a brief instant this woman didn't know what to do.

She didn't know whether to sit there and ignore me or to do what I had told her to do. She probably figured she didn't have anything to lose, since she was already helpless and getting worse.

I said to her one more time, "Sister, the Lord is telling me in my heart that I am to tell you to do something. If you will do what I tell you to do, I believe your healing will *begin* in a matter of seconds. In the Name of Jesus, be healed! Start getting up out of that chair and take your first step."

Something registered. This was her hour...her moment...her time to be healed. Somehow a *knowing* came in her that she and I were SUPPOSED to be having this experience together, and at that exact moment and place. I felt it. She felt it.

She let out a little cry and leaned forward in that kitchen chair. I was close enough to hear the bones in her back begin to crack and pop. I whispered, "Start coming out of there, in the Name of Jesus."

There was an audible gasp from the crowd and most of them jumped up to see what was going to happen. She slowly moved her right foot until it was pretty squarely placed on the floor. And then the other foot. And then like some invisible hand was causing her to rise, she just STOOD UP.

She didn't stand very steadily. It looked like she might have to sit down in the chair. I wouldn't have minded if she had. We would just have started over again. I whispered, "In the Name of Jesus, take a step toward me."

And a look came over her face that I'll never forget. Her face was FILLED with that determined look of faith. She began to move her feet, first scooting them a little on the floor, and then finding that she could raise both knees and feet a little at a time.

Well, the next part I can't describe clearly because pandemonium broke out. Suddenly, she was walking off the

16

platform and down the aisle. People were crowding around her to look at her, to touch her, to talk to her. Other people were raising their hands and praising God. Some were so excited they were jumping around because they were being healed at the same time.

And Oral Roberts was standing there saying to himself, "Thank You, God, that I told her to do what You told me to tell her, and that she did it, and that You are causing her miracle to start."

This woman lived only a few miles from Tulsa, so I was able to follow her continued growth into whole health. In a few weeks' time she was a well woman again. She grabbed onto that burst of healing and went on with it.

Now, what would have happened if I hadn't told the woman what Jesus told me to tell her?

What if she had disobeyed or had just flat out refused to do anything?

I'm convinced that she would have become worse.

And that brings me to you today.

God has told me to tell you:

> "IF YOU WILL DO WHAT I TELL YOU TO
> DO, A MIRACLE WILL START HAPPENING
> IN YOUR LIFE."

How do I know God told me that?

Well, I've come to know His voice.

How can you know that God speaks to me?

Well, I've got to ask you, "Do you believe the Bible? Do you believe that Jesus ever spoke to anybody in the Bible? Do you believe He's the same today?"

If you say no, then there's nothing I can do to help you. But if you believe that God ever spoke to people and that He's the same God as He's always been, and that He speaks today, then you can believe that God has spoken to me.

I *KNOW* He speaks. And I seldom act hastily on it. I

17

carry it in my heart. I ponder things. I don't rush off the deep end. I know God told me to take His healing power to my generation. I held it in my heart 12 years and when He told me to move, I did it.

I know He told me to build Him a university, and I carried it in my heart over 20 years until he told me *when* to do it. And then I did it, along with many associates and Blessing-Pact partners who joined with me. Come to Tulsa and you can see it.

God told me to build the City of Faith Medical and Research Center.

I held it in my heart to merge His healing streams of medicine and prayer – the natural and supernatural.

When He said to move, I did. We've got it up and operating. Come to Tulsa and you'll see it. And if you become a patient here, you'll experience the merging of medicine and prayer like God told me…and your hopes, I believe, will increase for a cure, a healing, better health.

How can you know that God is using me to say to *you*:

> "IF *YOU* WILL DO WHAT I TELL *YOU* TO
> DO, A MIRACLE WILL START HAPPENING
> IN *YOUR* LIFE."

Well, you're not going to know that for sure unless you actually DO what I tell you to do. This book can sit on your shelf and mean absolutely nothing in your life – and nothing to help you get better health and prosperity. Unless you *do* what I tell you to do.

You can sit and ask yourself forever, "I wonder if a miracle would happen to me if I did what Oral Roberts has told me to do."

The only way you KNOW that God told me to say that to you is if you choose to *DO* something about it.

That's why I'm writing these words to you. I'm going to tell you some things that God has told me to tell *you* to help you get well. This book is a message God has for *you*.

If you do the things I tell you to do, I am completely convinced that you can have better health.

Are you listening?

Do you have a listening heart?

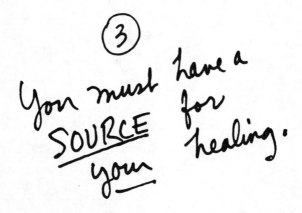

3

You must have a SOURCE for your healing.

Through what some people would call coincidence, but what I would call the providence of God, Harry and I met one day. He was a Vietnam veteran, the nephew of one of my dear partners. Harry's aunt had been praying earnestly for him and for his total healing. We found ourselves in the same room one afternoon, side by side.

As I looked at Harry I noticed his left arm had a brace on it, and his fingers were in a leather stall. He was bent over like he was shielding his back, and he had a rather vacant look in his eyes.

Harry looked up at me as I stood near him. He kept his eyes on me for what seemed like at least a minute or two. Then very slowly he got to his feet and forcefully got his balance.

I said to him, "What's the matter?"

To my surprise, he called me by my name. He said, "Mr. Roberts, I'm not going to make it."

"What?"

"I'm not going to make it."

"What's the matter?"

"Well, when I was in my last battle in Vietnam, shrapnel burst all around me. It struck my shoulder and almost tore it off. I was lucky that the helicopters picked me up and rushed me to the surgeons, who did a fantastic job on my shoulder. But as they operated, they inadvertently cut a nerve."

"What happened then?"

"I began to lose the feeling in this left arm until the feeling now has gone out of my fingers. My left leg is numb clear down to my foot. My back hurts terribly. I'm not going to make it."

"How did you know my name?"

"I've been in hospitals in California for several weeks now. As I was lying there with time on my hands, my aunt came and read some of the letters you had written to her. Then one day it dawned on me I wasn't getting well. And I thought of you."

I said, "Harry, tell me about it."

He said, "When I was a little boy back in Texas, I watched you on television. And the other day I tuned in to one of your prime-time specials because of the guest stars you had. I saw Richard, your son, and the young people from Oral Roberts University with you also. And then I saw you, and I immediately knew you were the one my aunt had been telling me about."

"Are you a Christian?"

"No, but I'm searching."

"Have you been searching for a long time?"

"No, not really. I was reared in church. But when I was

21

shipped to Vietnam I put all that behind me and really never thought of God again."

"Not ever?"

"Well, not much. However, I really began to think as I lay there on my hospital bed."

"What did you think about?"

"Mr. Roberts, all I could think of was I had to have help."

"But you were getting medical help."

He said, "Yes, and I was getting the best. But I wasn't getting well."

As he said that, I began to know deep in my spirit what to say next. I said, "Do you know what to do *now*?"

He said, "No, I guess not."

I said, "There's a little prayer in the Bible that goes like this: 'O God, be merciful to me, a sinner' " (Luke 18:13).

Then I did exactly what I usually do in cases where there is a compelling mood upon me to do something that I feel directed of God to do. Without asking his permission, I said, "Please join your good right hand to mine, and repeat this prayer after me. 'O Lord, be merciful to me, a sinner.' "

Before he seemed to realize what he was doing, he was repeating the words. As he said the words, his hand gripped mine and I knew that he was doing business with God.

I had him say the prayer again after me, and then I had him say it by himself. He looked up at me. "I feel different," he said.

"How do you feel?"

"Well, I just feel God."

"How do you know it's God?"

"It's a feeling of peace all over me."

"Well, that's what I call the presence of God."

Then I said, "Harry, in a few moments I want to pray for your healing. But first I want to say something to you very directly."

"What is it?"

I said, "Harry, you need to make God the Source of your life, as well as receive Him as your Savior as you have just done. You told me you grew up in the church, but after going to Vietnam you put God and all that behind you. You said you really put God out of your mind. That means when you went into battles you went without a sense of God being with you. Harry, you had no *Source* for your life. And everybody must have a Source."

He said, "What do you mean, a Source?"

"Well, you know that water has to have a source. And when you cut off the source, the water stops. The same is true with light in your house. It's connected to the power company, which is the source for it. If you disconnect the source, then your lights won't burn."

He said, "Yes, that's right."

I said, "In the same way, you've got to think of your life as being connected with God in a way that you know He is the Source of your life and of life *more abundantly*, as He has said in the Bible. And, Harry...

A SOURCE IS *NOT* AN INSTRUMENT.

He said, "What do you mean?"

"I'm telling you this...there are many instruments on this earth that you can turn to in order to get your health moving in a better direction. You can turn to medicine or prayer or both together. You can turn to exercise or a better diet. Sometimes a new job or a new climate will help. These are tools...instruments...methods.

"But if I had a hammer and I could drive the nail through the board and brad it to the other side of your understanding, I'd get this message into you. These things are *not* sources."

23

YOU'VE GOT TO MAKE GOD THE SOURCE OF YOUR LIFE AND OF YOUR HEALING.

That's one of the most important things I can say to *you*. There is only one Source for healing and health for you. There is only one Source for everything good you and I can know in this life. He is God... God is the SOURCE.

True, God works *through* instruments. He uses many different instruments or methods to bring us *into* better health. But, friend, He isn't *limited* to any one of them... he is above them all. He uses different methods – and different *combinations* of methods – for different people at different times in different places. He alone is the SOURCE.

We must always begin with God. He is our Source. This book is an instrument. Oral Roberts is an instrument that God can use in your life. You are an instrument. But there is only one God and He is the SOURCE of all life and all healing.

Oral Roberts has God as his Source. Harry made God his Source that day – you've got to do the same.

And then I asked Harry to do something very specific...

④

The Way God works is based on the seed. You must do things the way God does them. Here's how...

"Harry, I want you to do me a favor."

Harry looked back at me in surprise.

"You want me to do a favor for you, Mr. Roberts? What can I do for you? Why do you need a favor from me?"

"Your doing me a favor has a great deal to do with your getting well today."

"What do you mean by that?"

"Jesus said in Luke 6:38, 'Give, and it shall be given unto you; good measure, pressed down, and shaken together, and running over...'"

"Harry, Jesus teaches in the Bible that you and I and everybody have a need to give, and we must give *first*. Then it will be given to us running over. He specifically told *us* to *start the action*. He said that giving starts with us. He calls it a *seed* that we plant, and it produces a harvest, or what I call a miracle."

"Well, I've never had a miracle in my life."

"You just had one."

"When?"

"Just a little while ago when God's peace came in your heart when you prayed the sinner's prayer."

He said, "You call that a miracle?"

I said, "The greatest miracle of all is your personal salvation and your making God your Source."

He smiled and said, "I have to admit I never felt like this before in my whole life. It feels great."

I said, "The main thing is that you keep that in your heart, and never let it get away. Your salvation is the miracle of miracles."

He looked at me and said, "Mr. Roberts, you asked me to do you a favor and give you something. Well, I don't have anything to give. The money I earned in Vietnam is gone. Part of my body seems permanently paralyzed. So why would you ask me to give you something when I don't have anything to give?"

"I'm asking you for a favor because Jesus said for you to *give*, and to *give first*."

"Well, what can I give you?"

"You can give me a prayer."

He was so struck by surprise he said, "Mr. Roberts, you have need of prayer even from someone like me?"

"Everybody has needs, Harry. You do. I do. Everybody has."

"Well, I don't know how to pray for you."

"Just put your hand on me, and say, 'God, bless Oral Roberts and help him.' "

"Right now?"

"Yes."

He stumbled through his very sincere prayer. "God, I

26

really don't know what to say to You about Oral Roberts. He says he has needs and I believe him. Please help him."

I thanked him and said, "Harry, the main reason I asked you to pray for me was far greater than my own need for it, although I have much need of prayer. I wanted you to pray for me because you had the *need to pray, then the need to receive* a prayer. I thank God for what the surgeons and also the nurses have done for you. They have saved your life. And now apparently only a miracle can do the rest of it. Since you prayed for me first as a seed you planted, I'm going to pray for you now."

He seemed to tense up and I said, "Harry, now this meeting is not an accident. You and I were supposed to have met through your aunt's letters, through the television program, and through this scene today. Do you believe that?"

He said, "I've got to believe it. It's just more than coincidence."

I held out my hands and said, "Look at me. These are just a pair of human hands. There's no POWER in them. The power is in God. But they can help you release all that faith you've had stored up in you for years."

He said, "Wait a minute. What do you mean, the faith I've had stored up in me for a lot of years?"

"Well, you have faith. Everybody does. The important thing is to get it released to God and send it up to Him."

He said, "How do I do that?"

I said, "When I put these two hands near your shoulder, your arm and your fingers, or even if I touch you, I want you to try to visualize the hands of the Lord Jesus Himself, rather than mine. The reason is, if He were standing here and He put His hands out to you, you probably would believe that you'd be healed."

He nodded that I was right.

"So when my hands are stretched out to you, try to think of them as an *extension of His hands*. You see, I'm

27

only an instrument. But He is the Healer. He is the Source."

Without waiting, I simply put my hands near him and asked God for a miracle. I said, "God, you know how to heal his shoulders, his hand, his leg, his fingers, his foot, his back, his *whole being.*"

When I finished my short prayer, the young man said, "Will you help me take this brace off?"

I said, "Don't you think you should let your doctor do that?"

But he said, "Right now I think it should come off, even if I have to put it back on later."

By this time he didn't need my assistance, and soon he had the brace off and was moving his shoulder up and down in rapid motions.

I said, "Do you have any feeling back in it yet?"

He said, "Man, it feels good. But the main thing is I wanted to see if I could bend and touch the floor, and then stand back up again."

As I watched, that's what he did.

Then he said, "I've been wanting to move these fingers. You see, these fingers have been shot and they're stiff. I want them to move."

Tears welled up in his eyes as he was able to move the fingers a little at first, and then better and better.

I said, "Harry, this is your beginning...only the beginning. You've found God as your Savior and as your Source for your life. You did that partly by opening up and praying for me and planting a seed of your faith. You asked God to help me, and that indicates that you are beginning to open yourself up to God and to life. Jesus said to give, and it shall be given to you. When you give to Him, you are *giving Him something to work with.* Do this continuously and continually. I call it your Blessing-Pact Partnership with God. And when you work with it, it works with you. Through it you can really expect miracles in your life. Because God is a God of blessing, and will be your life's Partner, you can have this Blessing-Pact Partnership with God all the days of your life."

He nodded and said, "Mr. Roberts, I've got to get back to the hospital. I want the doctors to give me a complete examination again."

I said, "That's what you should do. I can tell you one thing, Harry. Whenever there's a miraculous healing, it will survive a thorough medical examination, and it will only make your faith stronger."

So he shook my hand with a firm grip. He turned and took a few steps, and then he came back. Looking straight at me, he said, "Mr. Roberts, I'm going to make it now. I'm going to make it now." And he turned and walked away.

Now let me tell you what this means to you and me today.

Let's get it right down where we can look at it together.

GOD HAS A WAY OF DOING THINGS

Harry learned God's way and you can, too. There's not a thing that you or I can do to *change* God's way. We've only got one choice: to do it His way or not to do it.

If you have it in your head that you can change God's way of running this universe, then you'd better close this book and never open it again. Because you *can't* change God's way of doing things.

But I tell you today...

You *can* LEARN God's ways.

YOU MUST LEARN GOD'S WAYS

Are you listening?
Do you have a listening heart?
One of the ways God does things is with...

THE SEED PRINCIPLE

Until I was 14, I lived on a farm and there's no better way to see life in the raw.

One of the basic principles I learned on that farm was what it took to have a *crop*. Now maybe you were raised in the city. Even so, you know that the groceries you eat come from seed that somebody planted, and planted *first*. A crop comes from seed. And the best crops come from the best seed.

You know that without even thinking any further. The fact is that the whole earth operates on the principle of seedtime and harvest.

God said to Noah and his family – who were the tenth recorded generation in the book of Genesis – just after they had survived the Flood and left the ark:

> "As long as earth remains...
> there will be *seedtime* and
> harvest" (Genesis 8:22).

It's been that way ever since. It's that way now, and it'll be that way as long as this earth remains. That's just the way it is. It's a principle of God. It's part of the way He arranged things.

You've got that straight in your mind, haven't you? You know that without even thinking any further.

Now this principle doesn't just relate to the farm. It's a principle that God uses in the entire Bible and in the entire human race today, including you and me as individuals. It's a principle that works in every area of our lives.

YOU MUST PLANT SEED TO GET A CROP!

Another way to say that is:

You have little reason to expect a crop or harvest if you *don't* plant seed. No farmer would sit watching for a field to sprout and grow if he hadn't planted anything. The two

30

are linked together – seedtime and harvest. When a farmer plants seed, he expects to reap a harvest from it. He doesn't expect anything if he doesn't plant. It's like the two sides of a coin.

It's like breathing.

Take a deep breath of air IN. And then breathe it out slowly.

Now if you don't breathe in again, you'll never breathe out. And if you don't breathe out, you'll never breathe in.

Breathe air IN. Breathe air OUT. (Do it now!)

It's the same with seedtime and harvest.

One is for the other.

The Bible says it like this in Galatians 6:7:

> "Whatsoever ye *sow*, that
> shall ye also reap."

Harvest – the reaping – is one of the basic principles of life...including your health...your finances...your relationships. Seedtime is followed by harvest.

Harry had *a need to receive a prayer*. So he had *a need to plant a prayer*.

Harry's aunt had a need to see her nephew healed. She had planted many seeds by praying and by giving first. By writing to me and by being a Blessing-Pact partner of my ministry, she had let *me* be involved in planting seeds of prayer and words of encouragement in Harry's life. I had prayed for him before I had ever met him.

By the time Harry and I met, the seeds had been planted. They had been growing for quite some time. We were at the moment of harvest.

Let me tell you that no matter how you and I may know Jesus as our Source and our personal Savior, or how much we understand that we have to plant seed in order to make things start to happen, we also have got to learn how to...

31

EXPECT A HARVEST

I've said it another way on television and in my crusade services for many years: "Expect a Miracle." It's one and the same thing.

I have spent many hours with our scientists here at Oral Roberts University in Tulsa, Oklahoma. Many of these men and women are about as skilled as you are going to find in this world. I've asked them – both on the under-graduate level and in the graduate schools – to explain *seeds* to me. I've talked to biologists and chemists and other scientists. Sometimes when they start explaining it all to me in those high-sounding scientific terms, I say back, "Just say it to me in plain language."

And when it comes down to plain language, this is what they say, "The bottom line on what makes a seed sprout and grow is that it's a miracle."

I have seen many people do everything right for their healing except at this one point – they have not under-stood that you have a *right* before God to expect to re-ceive from what you have planted.

I don't know why some people feel guilty about receiv-ing a harvest unless they have been taught incorrectly in the past, or have had bad experiences in their background.

We are *supposed* to receive. If you don't receive, God is not pleased, you can never be pleased, and the very thing that God wants you to have, you probably won't ever get.

WHEN YOU PLANT GOOD SEED IN GOOD SOIL YOU CAN <u>EXPECT</u> TO RECEIVE A GOOD HARVEST!

Are you getting this basic principle of the Blessing-Pact Partnership into your mind? Let it soak in...and soak in deep. It can mean all the difference in your getting well.

There's something else very important about seeds and harvest that you must choose to know...and you must have to know...

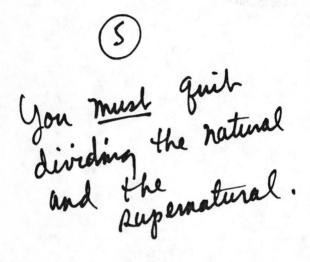

5

You must quit dividing the natural and the supernatural.

"A miracle is a miracle is a miracle."

I've said that to people for years. And I say it to you boldly today.

You are a miracle. It's a miracle that you were ever born. It's a miracle that you are alive today. You may never have thought of it that way, but you have to admit it's true.

The very idea that you were born when you were born...in that exact place...in that exact circumstance...and all the years from then to now until this very moment you are holding this book in your hands...

Why, it's a miracle!

Your body is a miracle. It's amazing how it works. Your

34

heart pumps blood, and your lungs take in oxygen, and your stomach digests food, and your nerves send messages...constantly...without your ever thinking much about it.

The fact that you are a living soul inside your body is a miracle. The way your spirit works with your body and your mind is a miracle.

And I want you to understand something today–just as if you had a blueprint laid out for you to see everything clearly:

> GOD DOES NOT SEPARATE THE
> NATURAL AND THE SUPERNATURAL
> IN YOUR LIFE.

Another way to say that is this...

THE SUPERNATURAL AND THE NATURAL ARE <u>ONE</u>

God doesn't separate them. He never has. He doesn't today. He never will.

He cares about you as a *whole*. He doesn't just care about your soul and ignore your mind and body. He doesn't just care about your body and ignore your mind and soul. He sees you as a whole.

Man is the one who decided that certain things were natural and certain other things were supernatural. Those are labels we've put on events and circumstances. God doesn't make that distinction.

Because God is in creation, a medicine might work in your body "supernaturally" just as prayer helps you get into better health as you release your faith. It's just as "supernatural" that a seed grows as it is that your finger can be sewn back to your hand and heal after it has been severed.

God made this earth and everything in it. He put all

35

the chemicals in the earth that man needs – in fact, He made man out of the chemicals. He knows every combination of chemicals that can make you healthier. He arranged it. He planned it. He put these chemicals together with certain principles. He didn't create part of the world and call it natural – and then create another part of the world and call it supernatural. He created it as a *whole*.

Now this may be a new idea to you. I'll come back to it again soon to help you grasp it fully in every part of your being...but you need to take it now as a basic principle that's crucial for your health.

There is no separation between the natural and the supernatural.

I know this is true because I've experienced it in my own life.

I personally have been without health for both brief and long periods of time. I have undergone surgery seven times. I've been under the care of doctors most of my lifetime. I've had people praying for me. But the principles I've talked about in this chapter have been at the heart of every HEALING I've ever personally experienced.

In 1977, God told me to make the most gigantic effort of my faith and calling and to build the City of Faith. It's the largest medical and research center *on one base in the world*. We opened it November 1, 1981. And its sole purpose is to merge God's healing streams of medicine and prayer to help people get well. As one fellow has said, "Oral Roberts has been through hell and high water, along with his partners and friends, to get the City of Faith built and opened."

How did we do it?

WE PLANTED SEED

We began with seed. I have in my office a piece of paper that lists the names of the men who were with me

36

the day I first announced to them the vision God had given me for the City of Faith. We each took out the biggest bill we had in our wallets and put it on the center of the table. And then we joined our hands in prayer.

WE CHOSE TO TAKE ACTION

The important thing is that we *did* something. We didn't just sit around and talk. We didn't just daydream. We did something concrete and real.

And then we recognized right away at the beginning that God would be the true Builder of the City of Faith.

WE KNEW GOD AS OUR SOURCE

We never thought for a minute that we could do it on our own. We knew He would have to work in the hearts of our Blessing-Pact partners so they could understand what we were doing. We knew that God would have to show us the specific plans and details for the buildings – and He did. He would have to give us strength–and He did. God was, and is, the SOURCE of the City of Faith. He gave the vision for it. He inspired us. He gave us ideas and abilities we didn't know we had.

WE WORKED AND EXPECTED A HARVEST

Now that doesn't mean we just sat around and waited for it all to happen. "Expecting" is *working*. A farmer doesn't plant seed, then sit down and wait. He waters...he cultivates...he harrows...he weeds...he is always working *in expectation, in anticipation,* of what is going to happen.

And, friend...we worked! Many times we had our backs to the wall, with no exit sign. And each time we planted more seeds. We worked a little harder. We never gave up, because we knew that God was the SOURCE

37

and that our *seedtime* would be followed by *harvest*.

We saw God use many different instruments. One of the instruments He used to build up my own faith was a vision of Himself. It came when I was so tired and feeling so alone and discouraged that I felt like going off and finding a hole to crawl into. He showed me in my inner vision that *He* was in charge. I saw our blessed Jesus much bigger than the City of Faith—a time and a half as big—lifting it up in His hands.

People laughed at me for saying I had seen Jesus 900 feet tall. (The problem was, I didn't see him *big* enough.) But that vision was an *instrument* that God used to build me up when I was so low that had I died you would have had to jack me up to bury me.

God worked in different ways in the lives of my associates who were helping me build the City of Faith. He worked in different ways in the lives of my Blessing-Pact partners as they planted seed after seed of their faith. He knew just what each person needed. We saw miracle after miracle as we moved toward the greatest miracle harvest of all: the opening of the City of Faith, although all the inside was not finished.

WE GOT A MIRACLE HARVEST

And we know it *is* a miracle. Everything about it is a miracle. If you come to see it here in Tulsa, Oklahoma, you'll say it's a miracle, too. We don't look and say, "See what we did over there in our hard work." And then look another direction and say, "See what God did over there." It's *all* a miracle. There is no difference in the natural and the supernatural efforts. It's a whole. And we've got to complete all the inside...and to OPERATE it daily...keep it going so the devil can never close it down –or change its character.

But you say, "That's fine and dandy, Oral Roberts, for you and the City of Faith. But what about me...this one lone person here in need of healing."

Well, that's the reason I shared with you about *principles*. A principle is a principle is a principle. Just like a miracle is a miracle is a miracle. God doesn't have certain principles for big projects and certain principles for people and certain principles for crops. He has *principles*. And the fact is:

> God has everything at His disposal to help you receive your healing and health, and the supply of your needs. He has everything we call *NATURAL* and everything we call *SUPERNATURAL*.

And you've got to take it *all*...and be thankful.

You must *not* close yourself to <u>*anything*</u> God may choose to use in helping you.

I know people who say, "I'll just trust God to heal me through prayer alone."

And I know other people who say, "I'll just go to the doctor and get well through medicine."

Both are equally wrong. The person who trusts in prayer alone is limiting himself to one method. So is the person who trusts only in medicine. People who think and act this way are failing to see that...

GOD DOESN'T PUT MEDICINE IN ONE BOX AND PRAYER IN ANOTHER BOX. THEY ARE NOT TO BE SEPARATED. THEY ARE TO BE INSTRUMENTS FOR <u>ONE WHOLE RESULT</u>: <u>YOUR HEALING</u>, <u>YOUR DELIVERANCE</u>.

Get them both.
Get the best you can.
Quit separating them.
Out in front of the City of Faith, just before you get to

the 60-foot high Healing Hands, we have two fountains that flow together into one gigantic healing river. Just like the Healing Hands, one of the fountains stands for medicine. The other stands for prayer.

But, friend, when the water from those fountains flows together, you can't tell the difference between the drops of water. You can't look at the river and say, "There go the drops that come from the fountain that stands for prayer," and then look over in another direction and say, "There go the drops that come from the fountain that stands for medicine." They are as *one* river of water.

The same is true for healing in your body.

Your faith can't tell the difference between the supernatural and the natural.

God doesn't make a difference.

Get all you can of GOD'S NATURAL METHODS FOR YOUR HEALING.

Get all you can of GOD'S SUPERNATURAL METHOD OF PRAYER.

And start doing it today.

Are you listening?

Do you have a listening heart?

GOD HAS A WAY OF DOING THINGS AND YOU NEED TO LEARN IT...

1.   GOD IS YOUR SOURCE. Everything else is an instrument.

2.   YOU'VE GOT TO PLANT SEEDS – and plant to get a crop. You've got to take action.

3.   When you PLANT IN GOOD SOIL, you can expect a good harvest.

4.   DON'T LIMIT GOD to any one instrument or method.

40

5. DON'T SEPARATE GOD'S PRINCIPLES into supernatural and natural.

6. START ACTING ON THIS NOW.

⑥

You must quit blaming God for the way things are in your life today...

"Why?"

It's a question I hear all the time.

"Why me, God?"

"Why did I get sick?"

"Why did this go wrong?"

"Why did I lose my husband (or wife)?"

"Why did my child die?"

"Why don't I have enough money to pay my bills?"

You can tie yourself up in knots with the question "why?"

And, friend, you'll never get a clear-cut single answer until you begin to understand some things about God and about this world. The GOOD NEWS is that we already understand *some* of the answer. And the more of the answer we get, the better we know what to DO to make things better and to get going toward more health.

Part of knowing "why" is in understanding that things happen over a period of time. They happen a little piece now, and a little piece later.

You didn't get sick or in trouble in a day.

There's something else you've got to understand: EVERYBODY is sick in some way. God showed me that as plain as day in 1947, right before He placed me into a ministry of preaching and teaching and praying for the sick. He showed me that *everybody* has a healing need and is hurting in some way. The illness in you may be financial. (Have you ever been sick in your finances?) It may be in your body. It may be in your relationships. It may be in your spirit or emotions. Everybody has a hurt. No matter what type of hurt and need we have, it keeps us from being WHOLE.

What I'm trying to say to you is that EVERYBODY can ask "why?" And that means me...

EVERYBODY can find answers. Everybody can deal with that question and move on into greater health.

Including you.

GOD PERFECTLY ARRANGED THE WORLD

The first thing you have to understand is that God created this world. He also arranged this world. And when God arranged it, it was *perfect*.

Every single part of God's creation worked like it was supposed to work. All of the chemicals were lined up in the right ways. Man's spirit was lined up with God's Spirit. Every single bit of man's body and the earth and the whole universe was in right order and all the parts were working.

When Adam and Eve sinned and disobeyed an outright principle established by God, they put a cog in the works. Things were humming along and suddenly a joint was pulled out of place.

ADAM AND EVE *DIS*-ARRANGED WHAT GOD HAD ARRANGED

They caused their spirit to be out of harmony with God's Spirit. And this entire world and all of mankind ever since was thrust headlong into a state of *dis*-arrangement. It's as if someone scrambled the puzzle. Or threw a stack of papers to the wind. Chemicals were thrown out of balance and out of alignment. Sickness came among us human beings.

THE DEVIL TRIES TO KEEP THINGS *DIS*-ARRANGED

And in the midst of the whole process is the devil. He took every ounce of man's *dis*-arrangement and proceeded to make it worse. Some people call the devil a "negative force." Some call him "an evil nature." I call him what the Bible calls him, and that's the *devil*. He exists. He's real. And his specialty is lies and diseases and mischief...robbery, destruction, and death. He's out to destroy you. He's out to capitalize on that *dis*-arrangement. He's out to make it worse. And he works hard at seeing you hurt. Cruelty and suffering and pain are his ball game.

Now that makes Oral Roberts mad. It should make you mad, too.

I know without a doubt that it made God mad, and it still makes God man. That's the reason He sent Jesus to the earth...to put things back into order.

You see, from the time Adam and Eve sinned, everything has been in trouble. Things are out of whack. We have *dis*-ease because that's the way the whole universe is…it's uneasy, groaning, crying out to be put back into the perfect way that it all was in the first place.

Man made a lousy decision and the devil took it and ran with it.

JESUS CAME SO WE COULD BE *RE*-ARRANGED BACK TO THE WAY GOD WANTS US

God set up a way for man to get himself back in line with God. It was a method. It was called a "sacrifice." And it had to be blood–because life is in the blood. A sacrifice was a symbol of man getting his attitude together and back in line with God's attitude. And through the years, the people who wanted to be in line with God made sacrifices of sheep and doves and pigeons and goats and cattle.

But the people never really understood God, or how to get themselves TOTALLY lined up with Him again, except for a remnant in each generation.

So God sent Jesus. He sent His *only* Son on a "blood mission" to earth. Jesus came on blood business.

He lived the only perfect life that has ever been lived. And then He was nailed to a cross in a bloody, hideously painful way so that He Himself could be the *complete*, *perfect*, and *final* Sacrifice. Jesus was the end of the sacrifice method. He poured out His blood so we'd have a way of getting into right relationship with God, once and for all.

Not too long ago, I tried to make a business deal with a man for a piece of work. And I was doing pretty good. I had the price even lower than I had thought I'd be able to get it.

And the Lord spoke to me and said, "Oral Roberts, you're trying to get the price too low. You're wrong."

45

I knew immediately I was making a mistake, and I changed what I was doing and paid him a really fair price.

And then God said to me, "Oral Roberts, I paid a price. It was a *high* price that I paid in having My Son die on the cross. But I knew what I was buying. And what I was buying was worth the price."

And, friend, *you* were what Jesus was buying. He paid the biggest price that's ever been paid for anything in the history of the world. And God said you are worth every bit of it.

Jesus paid the price so you can get into right relationship with God. He paid the price so you can get your life put back into the arrangement that God had planned for it in the beginning. In the prayer that Jesus taught us to pray–commonly called the Lord's Prayer–He has us saying, "Thy will be done in earth as it is in heaven " (Matthew 6:10).

Every time you and I pray, "Father...thy will be done on earth as it is in heaven," Jesus is trying to help us think and believe and expect for God's *re*-arrangement to begin in us IN THE NOW...HERE ON EARTH WHERE WE LIVE TODAY.

Jesus is having us actually pray for heaven's best to join earth's best, and that it begin here.

Heaven's will is the way things are done in heaven. Of course we're not in heaven yet. But we are on the earth where God wants heaven's will done exactly as it is in heaven.

In heaven there is no lack...no sickness and disease...no poverty...no hurt in our relationships...no separation from our Heavenly Father.

Listen, friend, Jesus is heaven personified. He came to show us what our Heavenly Father is like...and all the saving and healing and supplying He did was to show us what heaven is like. And He told us to pray, "Thy will be done on earth as it is in heaven."

Before we get to heaven there is an appointment you and I have, and that is to die (Hebrews 9:27). And we will keep this appointment, that split second when the devil will touch us the last time, and we will be "absent from the body and present with the Lord" (2 Corinthians 5:8). There we will await the Resurrection when we shall be changed from mortality to immortality, from corruption to incorruption (1 Corinthians 15:53, 54).

You say, "Oral Roberts, what does this mean to me?"

It means that (1) between now and your appointment to die, Jesus is alive and active in your life if you choose Him to be. He is the resurrected Son of the Living God, returned in the power of the Holy Spirit to indwell you by His Spirit (1 Corinthians 6:19, 20). It means that (2) as you read...study...and HEAR His word, your faith will come forth to believe for a mighty FORETASTE of the things in heaven that Jesus made it possible for you to have (as God's will) on this earth.

And, friend, that includes your health, your prosperity, good relationships with family and friends, right relationship with God, your emotions under the control of your faith, etc.

Jesus paid the price "in full" for you—and for all these things—on Calvary. He knew you and what you are worth (even if you yourself are only beginning to know now!)

Therefore, for every time you blame God by saying, "Why has this happened to me?" you've got to stop it. God didn't design these bad things. They are of Satan and you must "resist the devil" that he may flee (yes, flee) from you (James 4:7).

The way the devil works through the choice and will of sinful man—to pollute this world, to *dis*-arrange the way God does things, to stop His will—is NOT God's way, but the devil's and man's.

Jesus is your way.

A missionary was being led through a thick overhanging

47

jungle when he saw the sun was blotted out. He cried to his guide, "How are we going to find the way out of here?"

Calmly the guide replied, "I am your way." And he was.

Jesus is the only Man Who ever dared to say and back it up, "I am the way, the truth, and the life" (John 14:6).

Jesus is your way to get things back into the right order. And you've got to turn your thinking and believing away from the way the devil does things and get them going in the direction of the way God does things.

You've got to say:

> "DEVIL, TAKE YOUR HANDS OFF ME. I'M GOD'S PROPERTY AND HE'S MAKING SOME PROPERTY IMPROVEMENTS IN ME!"

You say to God:

> "I accept the work that Jesus has done. I accept Him as the blood sacrifice for me. I accept His death and resurrection as the new way for me to get into right relationship with You. I accept His death as the way for things to start getting back into the way You want them to be...just like heaven...and I'm going to do everything I can do to get my life in line with You, and I'm going to do what You show me to do. I don't want EVER to go back to the way things were in my life."

When you do that, you've done a lot.

You've said, "I'm going to be *re*-arranged. God is going to begin to *re*-arrange me back to the way He wanted me all along."

You've just opened up a way so that God can...

> put back on you what the devil took off you,
> take off you what the devil put on you,
> put in you what the devil took out of you,
> take out of you what the devil put in you.

48

You've entered a new way of living. You've made it possible for God to begin to *re*-arrange you back to a perfect design. Think of you having this new beginning!

Are you still with me?

Are you listening?

Do you have a listening heart?

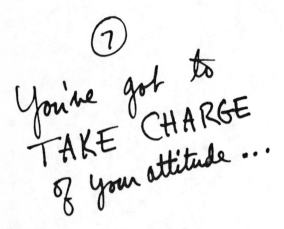

7
You've got to TAKE CHARGE of your attitude ...

Bob DeWeese! My associate since 1951. How I love him.

But there was one thing about Bob that "bugged" me for years.

Since his father died with a heart attack at 67, Bob got it in his head—or heart or both—that he would never live past his father's age.

"But, Bob," I protested, "your mother is in her 70's and healthy."

Later I'd say, "She's in her 80's and healthy."

Still later, "She's 90 and still going strong."

Bob's attitude was, "I know, I know. But I'm taking after Dad, not Mother. I'll die at 67 or before."

"Bob, you are stronger than I am, than most people I know. You were an Olympic swimmer. You are still a good athlete in your 40's."

Later I would say, "In your 50's."

Then: "In your 60's."

Bob would laugh. "Oral, I'm a Dutchman from Kansas. You know I have a hard head, and this is the way I think."

"But, Bob, you're a Christian before you're a Dutchman (or any other nationality). You and I are in a team of people who are in healing evangelism. We're working in God's system, not merely in man's. We have chosen to take control of our attitudes. That puts us in a *Take-Charge Position*, at least enough of the time to change things and to make things happen."

One day about three years ago, I got a call to come to the hospital. Bob, at 67, was down with a heart attack. Then he had a cardiac arrest and only the hard-working and alert doctors, with their fantastic machines, and with friends praying, brought him back. Bob actually left his body and saw the edges of heaven and started to enter it...when someone called him back.

But never mind, nothing really changed. I went to the hospital and Bob's wife, Charlotte, got the doctor to let me go in to see him. Bob was happy as a lark. He had worked with me as my co-evangelist in the large crusades, had been a pastor, had done a great work, and now he was ready and *eager* to go to heaven.

I prayed, and as I left I didn't feel a release in my spirit. I wasn't depressed about Bob's homegoing, but tugging deep in my heart was Bob's attitude. It was his attitude to *choose* the pattern of one parent who died 25 years BEFORE the other.

I'm not saying we can always reverse the direction in following our forebears. I *am* saying that there was more to Bob's situation than met the eye. But it was his life, and I loved him and was his friend all the way.

As I thanked the doctor and nurses and neared the elevator, I saw Bob's 18-year-old granddaughter who had grown up in our crusades, sitting with her mother or grandmother on the front seat of the big tent or auditoriums, hearing her granddad preach, hearing me and watching me as I prayed strong prayers to God for the sick.

Unknown to me, she was highly displeased that I had not prayed any stronger with her granddad a few minutes earlier. As I passed, she said, "Oral Roberts, you didn't pray a tent prayer for my granddad!"

I said, "This is not my hospital or where I'm in charge. I did the best I could. Besides, your granddad's attitude is set."

She said very frankly as the tears rolled, "But I sat on the front seat of your crusades in the big tents as a little girl. I heard you pray. I saw God heal people. And you're not doing it today for my granddad like you did then."

I stood there remembering.

She started to break down. Clutching my arm, she nearly bawled. "Please! Go back in there and really *pray* for my granddad!"

The Spirit moved in me and I turned and asked the doctor to let me pray again.

When Bob saw me, he said, "Did you forget something?"

"Almost," I answered.

"What was it?"

"My tent prayer."

He was puzzled. I said, "I mean I'm going to pray for you like I used to for people who came for healing prayers in our tent crusades."

He smiled. "That was something, wasn't it?"

"Bob," I said, "Cindy is upset. She remembers. Above all, she remembers the God who worked through you and me. Not just the words, but the anointing that breaks the yoke of sickness, sin, fear, poverty, and everything else that's not of God. She remembers."

He seemed genuinely puzzled until I said, "How old was your dad when he died?"

"You know, Oral, he was 67. You are not thinking of that, are you?"

"Yes, I am. How old are you now?"

"67."

"How old was Grandmother DeWeese recently when she went to heaven?"

"92."

"92?"

"Yes."

"And you chose your dad's genes over hers?"

"Now, Oral."

"OK. Let me ask you some questions. If you're happy with the answers, I'll get out of here and let you go."

I had his attention. "Ask me," he said.

"In your heart of hearts, have you finished what God called you to do?"

"I think so."

"But are you sure?"

No answer.

"Directly or indirectly, have you chosen to die at your father's age? In all these years you've mentioned this to me, have you been holding on to a wrong attitude?"

"Maybe. I'm not sure."

"Tell me as one of the closest friends you've ever had, do you trust me?"

"With all my heart."

"OK. It just may be that 67 is your year of appointment to die. It just may be that your genes and your father's are alike. *Or* it may be that God is not through with you and you can change your attitude and decide to be like your mother."

Bob looked at me sharply. We both were in uncharted

territory. The medical people were doing their job as it presented itself to them. I was doing mine, too.

"If you are willing, I will pray again, but not like before. Since I'm not a doctor, or one who knows scientifically about genes, I'll have to pray this prayer exactly as I feel it inside me. Then God can do what He pleases. At least, I will have done all I can do and also I can face your grand-daughter." Under my breath I added, "And God."

"Well," he said slowly. I guess we have nothing to lose."

"Hold on, Bob. It's a yes or no. It's a go or no-go. You know, and I know, there are times when a man of God speaks or prays and it's like Jesus doing it. Things happen!"

"How well I know," he replied.

I didn't know it at the time, but nearly a dozen doctors and nurses were watching from a distance. Since I was alone with Bob, I never thought of anyone else.

"Go ahead," he said.

My prayers for the most part are brief, and very much to the point. Often they are only one or two words. I heard myself say, "Bob, do you choose your father's genes or your mother's genes?"

Faintly he said, "Mother's."

"Say it so I can hear you!"

"MOTHER'S!" And he began to laugh that big infectious laugh of his. "But I've already been to heaven. I'm not sure I don't want to go back at this time."

"OK," I said. "I'm gone."

"No, wait!"

"Bob, I'm not going to impose anything on you, certainly not my own desires..."

"Oral, I know you when you get like this. I can feel your spirit. You're serious, aren't you?"

"Very serious."

"Do it!" he said.

54

I prayed: "Jesus, Bob DeWeese has chosen his mother's genes. He wants to live beyond that hang-up he's had for years over his father's death. I ask You, GRANT IT, in Jesus' Name! Amen and amen."

As I turned to leave, Bob's body began to shake and roll off the bed. Charlotte had slipped into the room, along with a couple of nurses.

They helped me roll his 6'3" body back on the bed.

Again, his body shook, but it was not a normal shaking. It was a shaking under the Spirit of God. The room seemed to fill up with light. I could feel enough heavenly power, I thought, to heal hundreds or even thousands. God was seemingly before us in His totally unlimited power.

When I left, Bob was hilarious. I left quietly and calmly.

As I passed Cindy, she smiled. "He will live. Don't worry. Those tent prayers still work."

"Cindy," I said, "it wasn't a tent prayer. Your mind as a little girl remembers prayers that were positive, prayers that expected results from a good God."

"Well, isn't God always a good God?"

I laughed. "You know He is."

Bob's recovery was good, and the doctors did their jobs well.

Later, I thanked one of the doctors for being so helpful to Bob. He said, "Something really happened in that room that day, didn't it?"

"Doctor," I said, "I can't prove it, but yes, it did. I don't know how exactly. Maybe there are depths of healing you and I and others may yet find that we've been looking for all our lives."

"Yes," he said. "Yes."

Bob DeWeese is alive and "healthy as a horse" at this writing some 3 years later.

Now I am not going to promise you or anybody else

what happened to Bob DeWeese. He will tell you that God healed him when he made the change in his attitude. What I *can* say to you is, I am totally convinced that God has put your attitude in your control. Not even the devil can take it from you, unless you let him. You can change your attitude for the better — sometimes that's a 180-degree change.

WHAT IS YOUR ATTITUDE?

You've heard people say, "Boy, he sure has a lousy attitude," or, "She has the worst attitude I've ever seen."

Or maybe it's been the opposite: "She has the greatest uplifting attitude I've ever known," or, "He's just great to be around—always has such a good attitude."

You know what an attitude is.

You may not be able to define it with lots of words, but you know that you have one and you know that everybody has one, and you know one when you see one.

I'm going to tell you some things about attitude. And the reason I'm going to tell you is so you can get control of your attitude before it gets control of you.

I'll say that again:

> *You're going to have to control your attitude, or it will control you.*

I'm determined to help you control it. Because if you let your attitude control you…there's no telling where you'll end up.

Now I want you to stop a bit and come to grips with that. Unless you're *willing* to try to harness your own attitude and say, "I'm going to take charge of my attitude"…there's no reason for you to go on with this book.

So get it decided.

You say, "But what does my attitude have to do with my healing?"

Just about everything.

Your attitude results in the choices you make. If you

make the same choices over and over, you form a habit. The stronger your habits become, the more you have a set pattern for living.

If your attitude is good...if it is on the side of God being your Source, and if it's based on the things God tells you to do...then you're going to make better choices. The better your choices, the better your habits, and the better your way of living.

And that includes your health
> your finances
> > your relationships
> > > your emotions.

So you've got to get control of your attitude.

You've got to say:

"I AM GOING TO CONTROL MY ATTITUDE."

Say it out loud.

Stand up and say it again.

Determine today—with every ounce of will that you can muster up—that you are going to take control of your attitude.

Because it's only when you decide to get control of your attitude that you can do what I'm about to say next...

（8）

You've got to trade in your poor attitudes for some better ones...

I'm going to share some things with you in this chapter that are very personal. They are right at the core of Oral Roberts. I'm not *eager* to share them with you, because they are so personal. But I'm *going* to share them because they can help you.

First, let me tell you where you got your attitude.

You learned it. Somebody taught you an attitude and you bought it. Or somebody tried to teach you, and you didn't buy it. You weren't born with an attitude. You *developed* an attitude as you grew up. It may have been a good one. It may have been a lousy one.

And what you've learned — you can *un*-learn. You can change your attitude. You don't have to think the way you always have. Your attitude hasn't been set in concrete somewhere. Not only CAN you change your attitude, but you OUGHT to change it. You ought to get it changed to be like God's attitude.

WHERE DO WE LEARN OUR ATTITUDES?

You and I got most of our attitudes from our parents and the people we grew up around.

I have laughingly said to many an audience, "The best thing I ever did was to choose my parents."

Of course you know I didn't choose my parents. I was born into my family without any choice. But the point I'm making is that I got extra blessed by the good God who saw to it that I was born a member of the Roberts family.

Papa went to heaven at 87, and Mama at 89. My brothers, Elmer and Vaden, are still alive and so is my sister Jewel. They are very dear to me.

They are dear to me beyond the fact that they are my blood relatives. They helped me choose a lot of the good attitude I have today.

I was born into a healthy family – the fifth and last child. My oldest sister, Velma, was a beautiful baby. She could sing almost like a nightingale as a little girl. Her mind was bright, her body was sturdy, and she was alert. She was just getting old enough to go to school when something went wrong. Nobody really knows what. Mama and Papa told me that over a period of weeks, she became an epileptic. She continued to get worse until her mind was affected.

Velma died at 19, not with epilepsy but with pneumonia.

In those days — and especially out in the country where we lived — we didn't have much medical help for pneumonia. I was only about two or three years old at that time. I really don't remember much about it.

But years later when I became ill with tuberculosis, there were folks who remembered Velma – and way back in their minds there was an attitude.

It went something like this: "When one of those Roberts children gets something in their lungs, it's the end. Velma died, and now Oral's going fast."

Now that attitude wasn't without a grain or two of fact to back it up. Velma *had* died. And Mama's father had died of a lung disease, too. Lots of folks in those days died of pneumonia, also of tuberculosis.

But the main thing about that attitude is this: it was a LOUSY one. It did absolutely NOTHING to help me get well. I had to fight that attitude with every ounce of energy I had.

Maybe you have an attitude that goes something like this:

"Well, arthritis (or any other
disease you want to name) runs
in my family. My mother had it
and my grandmother had it, so I
guess I'm going to get it, too."

or

"A lot of people in our area seem
to be getting cancer. I'll probably
get it, too, sometime."

or

"My father had a weak heart and since
he did, I'll probably have heart
trouble, too."

If you have an attitude like that—
STOP IT.

Change it. Get rid of it. It will do absolutely *nothing* to help your health or to start the healing process for you.

There were some other people in our part of the country that had a slightly different approach. They said to themselves—and not always very quietly, I might add:

"TB. Not much hope for that.
Guess Oral isn't going to be

with us too much longer."

And that wasn't without a little bit of fact, too.

More than 90 percent of the people who went to the sanatorium for tuberculosis in those days never walked out of there. Mama and Papa were both part Indian, and tuberculosis was especially rampant among the Indian people in Oklahoma where I was born. Thousands died.

But that didn't make it a good attitude. It did absolutely nothing – and I mean a big ZERO – in helping me believe God, or believe I was going to get well again.

And some of the people didn't even have to *say* anything. They'd just give me that pity look. I knew what they were thinking: "Poooooooooor Oral."

I see that look in some people today.

Some folks whisper like something is a big secret:

> "Did you know she has cancer. Isn't it just awful? I wonder how long she has to live?"

> or

> "Heart attack. You know, you never really get over it. Poor dear."

STOP IT!

If I could say it a million times to you, until it filled every cell in your being, I would.

STOP IT!

STOP IT!

STOP IT!

STOP IT!

Don't let that attitude take root in you. If you hear it, don't buy it. Don't spread it to others. That attitude will pull you down and slow you up until you'll be flat on your back, paralyzed in your spirit.

And while I'm at it, I'm going to share another lousy attitude that affected my life in those days. I'm going to get them all out. You may have been taught these attitudes, too.

Now this wasn't an attitude that *my family* had at all. But a lot of good church people had the notion that:

"If you trust God, you don't need a doctor."

I don't know where they got that attitude. I don't know just how it came to be so emphasized. But it was there.

The Bible says, "They that are sick need a physician." If you haven't read that, you just look it up. It's in Luke 5:31.

Now that seems pretty plain to me.

Actually what these church folk were doing–even though they may not have thought about it this way–was that they were dividing up God's methods and picking out the ones they liked best. They said to themselves, "I like only the method of prayer." And they limited themselves to that. (They were dividing up the natural and supernatural...which isn't what God does!)

In a way, they were telling God what to do. They were saying, "Now, God, if You want to heal me, then here's the way You should go about it – the instrument You should use."

Can you imagine trying to tell God *how* to heal someone? As if you know as much as He does. Well, they did. And lots of people still do that today.

They don't know that doctors are used by God. Medicines are used by God. And thank God, prayer is used by God. Sometimes a different diet or an exercise program, or a different climate are used by God. God doesn't make any difference between the natural and supernatural because He made them and combined them. They are all HIS methods and HE uses all of them.

If you think you don't need a doctor...

If you think you shouldn't take the medicines you need (which are chemicals from the earth that the Lord has made for you)...

If you think you don't need to pray and to receive heal-

62

ing prayer...

Then you need to change your attitude.

The attitude you have is going to hurt or completely destroy you...so you might as well trade it in on an attitude that will help you.

I LEARNED GOOD ATTITUDES, TOO

Now as I said to you before, my family didn't have that attitude. Papa was a strong believer in medical science even when he later became a minister of the Gospel. When I took ill, Papa and Mama called in the best doctors they knew. At the same time, they started praying and calling the people of the church to pray. They helped me develop a good attitude about that. They taught me the attitude:

GET ALL THE HELP YOU CAN GET

Get medical-science help.

Get prayer help.

Get Word of God help.

Get a change of attitude.

Get it *all*.

Don't be afraid of prayer. Don't be afraid of medicine. Get it all and get it going today in your life.

Don't wait. Don't make excuses. Don't delay.

I bless my family, especially, for teaching me a lot about a good attitude toward God – that He was my focus for *all* healing power.

Elmer, my oldest brother, left home when I was just a boy. He started looking for a job when times were tough and jobs were scarce. But Elmer held on until he got a job. And when he got work, he gave it his best. He worked *hard*. He still does. I learned an attitude from him:

DON'T EVER GIVE UP.

DON'T QUIT WORKING.

And you don't slow down, either, if you're going after something important that God wants you to have (like your health and prosperity!). You keep going on and keep going on until you get it.

My brother Vaden is only two years older than I am. We grew up like twins and were extremely close. When I collapsed with tuberculosis and was brought home by my coach, and Papa laid me down on the bed, Vaden fell across the bed with tears streaming down his cheeks. He said, "God, put it on me. I've always been stronger than Oral. Put it on *me*, God."

I tried to push him away because I didn't know what he was doing but Vaden really was saying to me that he cared for me. He wanted to take my place. In a sense, he was being like Jesus.

Vaden also believed that things have to be made to happen. There wasn't anything he wouldn't do for me. The doctors prescribed a diet of raw eggs beaten up in milk – and that was almost my only food for five months. Many times Vaden made up that mix of egg and milk for me. He made me drink it. He wasn't going to let me get away from his best attitude:

DO EVERYTHING YOU CAN DO!

And I learned a lot from Jewel, my sister, too. She was the only girl left in our family after Velma died. She was pretty special to all of us.

Jewel was different from us boys in that she was quieter. She kept things to herself more. But there was one thing Jewel had done at that time that none of the rest of us children had done. And that was to make a personal commitment of her life to Jesus Christ. She had already recognized that God was the SOURCE of her life.

Jewel had made some poor decisions before that. They had caused some pretty deep hurt and sadness in our family. But Jewel's attitude helped change the bad to good. She said, "Well, Papa and Mama and the rest of you, I've made some poor choices. I can't take them back. They're done. But now I've made a good choice. I've made a commitment to Jesus. I'm going to follow Him. And I'm going forward in my life."

Mama spoke up and said, "Jewel, we forgive you and we love you." And all of us felt the same way.

I learned a lot from Jewel. In fact, the good attitude that I have today I first started learning from her.

Jewel showed me that...

YOU HAVE THE POWER TO CHANGE YOUR ATTITUDE FROM BAD TO GOOD TOWARD JESUS CHRIST

You *can* make a personal commitment to Jesus Christ no matter what you may have done. You *can* make the best of a situation and turn the bad around to a greater good. You *can* have a better life than you have today. It's up to you.

YOU CAN HAVE A BETTER TOMORROW.
DON'T EVER GIVE UP.
DO EVERYTHING YOU CAN DO.

You have the power to turn away from all the bad attitudes that you have learned and trade them in on good attitudes. You have the power to choose new attitudes. You have the power to learn new attitudes.

I'm here to help you...

(9)

Here's how I took charge of my attitude to correct the worst mistake of my life. And if I could do it in the shape I was in, YOU can do it today!

As I've already told you, Oral Roberts has been down the road and through deep waters when it comes to sickness and health. And in the midst of that was the worst mistake I've ever made. You might be making the same mistake. If you are—and you aren't willing to start doing something about it, you might as well get yourself another book.

What was that mistake?

It was a failure to understand that God is a *good* God.

How did I make that mistake? How did I fail to understand for so long?

I grew up in a home where both my mother and father came to trust in God and began to teach me many right things about God while I was still just a boy. But I either caused myself to ignore God and what they were teaching me – or I just flatly "dumbed out."

How did that happen?

Well, let me say first that I was a little older than my years. I was what you could call a "fast bloomer." By the time I was 17, I was going on 30.

And I got it into my head to get out of my parents' lives and away from the teachings of God and the Bible and get out into the big unknown. I wanted to find a place where I could dream my dreams and make them happen.

You ask, "What did you dream about, Oral Roberts?"

Well, I wanted to be an athlete. And I wanted someday to be a lawyer–and then a judge and then the governor of the state of Oklahoma. I was dreaming of being governor, but my chances of being governor of Oklahoma were slim, and none, and slim had just ridden out of my little town.

I wanted to get away from poverty and what I saw as a dead-end street for my life out there in the hills of Oklahoma.

I saw that the church folks were good people, said good things, and kept the Bible at the center of their lives. But I never got the feeling that they were going anywhere. I didn't see God doing anything very *good* for them. I was burning to get an education – to get through college and on to a doctor's degree. (Back then folks didn't think much about going to college.)

Now you may think that it is the most normal thing in the world for a 17-year-old boy to leave home and to begin to make his dreams happen.

But I can tell you that it is the craziest thing in the world when *any* person tries to do *anything* on his own without dealing with God first.

The crazy part had to do with my attitude.

There was nothing wrong with my leaving home at 17,

if that was really what I was supposed to do. Nor was there anything wrong in my wanting to be an athlete. It certainly wasn't wrong for me to dream of following in the footsteps of my grandfather, who was a judge in Indian Territory days here in Oklahoma. Nor was there anything wrong about dreaming of being governor of Oklahoma.

No, there was nothing wrong with the *dreams*.

It was something wrong with my attitude about how I was going to get those dreams.

I had ignored God as a fact of existence in my daily life. I had left Him out of my dreams. I had failed to understand the basic of all basic facts:

GOD IS GOD.

And God has to be dealt with. He is God for Oral Roberts and He is God for every other human being – including you.

I left home. I gave my best shot to my dreams. I ran away to a neighboring town and entered school there. I was the tallest man and the highest scorer on the basketball team, so I became the captain – the one to lead the team. I moved in with a judge, and in the evenings I studied his law books on the side while I was still going to high school. I got a job at the little newspaper in that town so I could make some money. I was determined to make life happen.

I'd get up at 4 a.m., build the fires in the judge's house, go to school, practice basketball, throw my paper route, write my newspaper column, and maybe even have a date. Then I'd come home to study (I loved to study and was an *A* student). I pushed myself to the very limits of my physical ability – and beyond.

I began to have chest pains, and sometimes at night I'd wake up in deep sweats. I tired easily. But I was excited by my new life and supremely confident. NOTHING was going to stop Oral Roberts now.

But something did.

Basketball is a rugged game – far more rugged than most people realize. It takes a lot of energy. And in the midst of the final game in the district basketball tournament, I collapsed. Bleeding at my nostrils, my lungs feeling like they were bursting from my body, I fell to the floor, unconscious.

The next thing I knew, my coach had me lying in the back seat of his car. I heard him say, "Oral, I'm taking you home to your parents." And we drove off into the night.

When we got back to Ada, Oklahoma, Papa helped the coach carry me in, and he sent for the doctors. Their verdict: tuberculosis.

The next few weeks were a bloody nightmare to me. Bloody because I almost hemorrhaged to death several times. A nightmare because I didn't have control of my attitude.

I didn't understand that God would have a hand in my life if I would only let Him. I was dying. And as my body got weaker and weaker, all I could see were my dreams slipping away. I had been pulled back down to zero and I was still losing ground. I was bitter.

I hated what was happening to me. And it didn't seem to me that there was anything I could do about it. I had lost control.

I was bedfast for five months. I lost 43 pounds. The papers were signed to place me in the sanatorium for tuberculosis.

A boy named Oral Roberts – a stutterer and now a tubercular – faced the possibility that he might never put his clothes and shoes back on again and go out to face life. My dreams lay in shambles and I lay in shambles.

Once I was flat on my back, people kept coming around to tell me that God is God. They painted such a picture of God for me that I pretty much decided I didn't care to ever know Him. They'd say things to me as they left that made me think, "God put this disease on me. He has my number and He finally caught up with me." I hate to say it, but most of these were church people – the so-called "saints" of the church.

THE WORST MISTAKE OF MY LIFE WAS IN EVER BELIEVING FOR A SECOND THAT GOD HAD MADE ME SICK

Even the pastor had this attitude. He had learned in seminary that God was only interested in my soul. So the minister had to convince me to give that part to God. But he didn't believe God had anything to do with the healing of a human body. His main line to me about tuberculosis was: "Son, be patient."

Now when your body is dying a lot faster than it's living, it's pretty hard to be patient. And it's especially hard for Oral Roberts to be patient with people who are telling him to be patient.

I was lying there so sick that I couldn't walk anymore without help, dreading the nights because of the cold sweats and the awful coughing and hemorrhaging that came from time to time, wondering many times if I'd ever see another morning.

You talk about thinking things over and trying to get things into perspective. I really did some thinking.

I admit that I wasn't ready to hear what Papa said to me one day. He said, "Oral, you've got to get saved, son, and give your life to God."

I didn't say anything.

And he went on, "Son, don't you know how sick you are? Don't you realize that the doctors have told me several times that, with the state of medicine as it is today, you're probably not going to live. Therefore, as your father and as a Christian, and now as a minister of the Gospel, I've got to see you saved and know that you're going to heaven when you die—which may be any day or night real soon."

70

I blurted out, "Papa, I don't want to go to heaven."

He said, "What do you mean, you don't want to go to heaven?"

I said, "I want to *live*. I want to fulfill some of my life and get some of my dreams realized. Papa, if God is half as good as you and Mama say He is, I've got a right to live. I've got a right to get well. I don't want to go to heaven now."

Now I don't know whether I should have said all that...but I did. And I'm glad I did, because it was a big part of my healing process.

Something jarred loose in me. It was the first move in getting my attitude turned around.

And, friend, I tell you that you're going to choose to come to that place, too, if you ever have a better chance at the best health you can have. You've got to say:

"I WANT TO *LIVE*."

And mean it.

The more I continued to lie there, the more I began to doubt the things I was hearing around me.

One of the things that I was smart enough to pick up early in life is that you don't believe everything you hear. I believe that all true faith begins with honest doubt. By that I mean, you can't be gullible. You've got to have some solid evidence for what you believe.

Where did I get my doubt?

Part of it came from my family. I grew up in a family that didn't take everything at face value. One of my father's favorite scriptures was Hebrews 11:1. He would quote it to me at my bedside:

"Now faith is the substance of things hoped for, the evidence of things not seen."

He'd always emphasize the words *substance* and *evidence*.

And then he'd say:

"Now as you know, my father, Amos Pleasant Roberts, was a judge. I've stood many a time in

71

the courtroom and seen him demand that evidence be brought forth before he would render a judgment. My father didn't render judgments by whim, or by influence of the lawyers, or circumstances around him. He looked for *evidence*. And if he didn't have the evidence, he had a way of putting off the trial until he got it."

Papa brought this home to my own health one day when he said, "Oral, I've talked to you a lot about the Lord. I've told you about my father. And I also know I've studied the Bible. And I want you to know that *evidence* is what the Bible is all about."

I said, "Papa, what are you trying to say to me?"

He said, "Oral, as sick as you are, you have to have some kind of evidence that the bed you're lying on would support your weight, or you'd be trying to get out of it right now."

I knew he was right.

"Now, God," Papa continued, "is going to give you the evidence that will get rid of the doubt you have. He'll give you the evidence that will cause you to have faith in Him and to get saved. I don't want you to be full of doubt. I don't want you to miss heaven. You've got to look around you and in the Bible and get some evidence for your faith to act upon."

I've always known one thing about my father. He was not a highly educated man, but he had a lot of common sense and a good understanding of the way God does things.

But I still doubted. And doubted. And doubted.

I doubted that preacher who told me to be patient. I doubted the church people. I even came to doubt that the medicines the doctors were giving me were going to work. I doubted that God even knew my name.

I began to sift through all of those things I had been hearing.

And then my doubt turned into a good "mad" in my spirit. I got mad at that preacher. I got mad at those people who were telling me that God was out to get me.

(Now I don't say these people were *intentionally* trying to do me harm. They were generally good people who had just been carried along, down the wrong river. But you know and I know that if someone cuts your head off – whether they *mean* to do it or not – your head still gets cut off. These people weren't telling me the right things. At least my attitude wasn't hearing the right things. And either way, I wasn't getting any help at ALL from what was being said.)

A slow boil started inside me that there was something WRONG when we begin to think God is mixed up in the diseases that come on our bodies. Or that God wants us to be so patient when we get sick. That's against every medical precept I've ever known about. It's against everything we have learned at the Oral Roberts University School of Medicine and the City of Faith and in my praying for sick people all over the world.

When something goes bad that can possibly be corrected, don't get patient about it! You JUMP to make things start to happen to correct the situation. Don't listen to people who tell you to be patient!

I doubted.

And then I got mad.

And I also started looking for some evidence.

Strangely enough, I believed in my family. They were evidence to me. They were people I could see, feel, touch, hear. I had never seen God. As far as I knew then, I had never felt Him. But out where I grew up, folks made their word their bond. Their *word* was something you could depend upon. It was easier for me to take the word of my family as evidence than it was to believe anybody or anything else.

I remember once when my bedroom was full of kinfolks

73

and neighbors, most of them carrying on with me about how God had made me sick. My mother got up out of her chair and with blazing eyes like only my little Indian mother had, she said, "Now I'm not going to put up with this any longer."

The room got real quiet.

And she said, "I've seen people get well when there wasn't any medical hope for them from man's point of view. I've seen God miraculously heal people, even through my own prayers when all other hope was given up. I've never believed that God goes around this earth picking out people to make them sick and die before their time like is happening to my son Oral."

And then she really let them have it.

She said, "Now you people start getting your thinking straight or I invite you to get up and leave my home and stay away from here until you can come and *encourage* my son, rather than drive him deeper into a wrong understanding about God. That bad understanding might be cause for his never getting well."

And then she said one last thing I'll never forget. "Whether my son lives or dies through this tuberculosis, I know that God is better than you are making Him out to be."

Well, let me tell you there were apologies on all sides. People were stumbling over themselves saying, "Oh, Mrs. Roberts, I didn't mean that," and "Oral, I apologize."

That little five-foot, 100-pound mother of mine had let out a spiritual war whoop. And I sort of had the feeling that most of those folks were thinking that they might lose their hair if they didn't straighten up.

I took what Mama said as evidence.

She was saying to me loudly and clearly:

GOD IS A GOOD GOD

74

And then I took what Papa was *doing* as evidence.

Papa would come and kneel at the foot of my bed. One night he said to me, "I'm going to kneel by your bed and pray until you get saved."

Mama and the nurse joined him.

Now I had been accustomed to hearing my parents pray all my life. I listened for awhile and my mind drifted away. And then I focused on them again. I heard Papa's voice, but I heard another voice deep inside me, too.

It was like, "Oral, Oral, Oral."

I looked at Papa. His eyes were closed and tears were running onto the floor. And as I looked, his face just seemed to fade away and in a moment there was the countenance of Jesus. A bright light seemed to envelope Papa's face, and I had all the evidence I needed.

The words just came rushing up in me. They pushed up out of my mouth and I fell back on the pillow sobbing, "Jesus, Jesus, save me."

Have you ever heard someone say, "My heart got in my throat"? Well, that's what it was like.

I prayed and I felt the presence of Jesus Christ enter my feet and up through my entire body. A joy filled me and I felt light as a feather. It was so exhilarating I felt I would burst. I had a sudden rush of energy and Mama and Papa and I danced around the room, crying and laughing at the same time.

When my energy subsided, Mama and Papa laid me back in the bed. But there was a shine on my face now. I had dealt God into my life. I knew He was *good* and I knew He was *my* Savior.

But...

There were still some doubts about whether He wanted Oral Roberts to get up out of that bed permanently. I didn't doubt Jesus as my Savior, but I still doubted Jesus as the Source of my healing.

Here's how evidence came to block out that doubt.

Jewel came to my bedside, leaned down, and took my hand in hers. Without a flicker of an eyelash and with a voice as firm as could be, she said seven words that still live in me today.

She said:

"Oral, God is going to heal you."

There was a quiet force coming up out of her, clothing her words with life, and I felt my insides turn over. I replied, "Is He, Jewel?"

"Yes, He is, Oral. He is going to heal you."

And I took that as evidence. I believed it.

Perhaps I was just beginning to absorb all that my parents had been trying to teach me about God for those many months. Perhaps the wheat was finally being separated from the chaff in my mind. Perhaps I had finally reached the place where I had enough evidence.

I believed it.

I believed God was God.

I believed I had a relationship with God.

I believed God was going to do something good for Oral Roberts.

You say, "But what about *me*, Oral Roberts? You are supposed to be helping *me*."

The important thing for you is that you–YOU–must, must, must, *must*, MUST come to a place where you can say from the bottom of your heart…

I BELIEVE GOD.
I BELIEVE GOD IS TOTALLY <u>GOOD</u>.
I BELIEVE I HAVE A RELATIONSHIP WITH GOD.
I BELIEVE GOD IS GOING TO DO SOMETHING GOOD FOR <u>ME.</u>

It may not come to you like it came to me…or it may. The *way* it comes is not nearly as important as the fact that it comes. You have to reach a place deep down inside you that you know that you know that you know that you know.

76

And the only way you're going to get there is to get some evidence. And take that evidence as convincing you that God is God, God is *GOOD*, God is going to do something *GOOD* for you.

In all my life I've never seen so many things start changing as quickly as they did after Jewel said, "Oral, God is going to heal you," and I believed He would.

Are you ready for these things?

Are you listening?

Do you have a listening heart?

These things can happen for you...and they can turn you on your way to health and prosperity like never before.

Get ready...

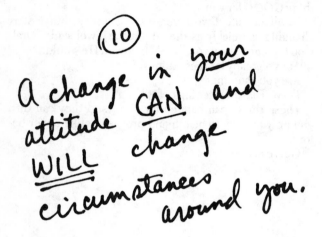

A change in your attitude CAN and WILL change circumstances around you.

God is God.

God is God in your life. He is God in my life.

Our God is a *good* God.

You've got to get that deep down inside you, get a better understanding of it, and never turn it loose the rest of your life. No matter what bad thing may hit at you, God did not cause it...and He wants you well.

Right at this point–whether or not you see this exactly as I see it–it is still OK. If you will just hang in there with me, the dawn is going to break, the clouds will lift, and you are going to get the most pleasant shock of your life. You're going to realize that God thinks more of you than you ever thought possible. Then you are going to rise up on the inside of your being and stand taller for the rest of your life. The devil is going to have a million times harder time bringing sickness and other bad things against you.

At the same time, God is going to have a much clearer way to start pouring His better health into you from the crown of your head to the soles of your feet. And the man writing this book has such a good feeling about you that I just can't wait to tell you what happened next in my own experience.

Things started happening.

And when I say happening, I mean HAPPENING.

Number One. The first thing that happened was a change in the attitude of my doctors.

I had three physicians—Dr. Craig, Dr. King, and Dr. Shi.

Each of my doctors had a different attitude on their next visit to see me. Now maybe it was just that I was able to feel their different attitude—but either way, our relationship was better.

You see, I had just about given up on taking medicines that these doctors had prescribed. As I lay in my bed, with people telling me I was going to die, and my attitude so negative that I was believing that I truly *was* going to die—I didn't see much point in doing what the doctors had said. That medicine tasted awful, and I decided it just wasn't worth taking if I was going to die anyway. (Do you see how bad my attitude had been? Your attitude can control you if you don't control it. Are you listening? Do you have a listening heart?)

But after I began to believe that God and I had a relationship—that God is a good God...that God is a God of health and wholeness...and that He cares about Oral Roberts—my attitude changed and that included my attitude about my doctors and the medicines they prescribed.

79

Doctors tell me, "We have to deal with sickness so often and so steadily that we have to be careful that we ourselves don't lose hope. We get impatient when better drugs aren't available, or new surgical techniques take so long to prove, or new innovations in hospital care take so long to be put into place. It wears us down and we have to struggle to keep our hope up for patients." Maybe that's what had happened to my doctors.

One thing I did know–I knew then and I still know today–is that my doctors were *for* me. Not a one of them had said what the preacher had said, "Son, be patient." All three of my doctors were trying with all the skill they had to get me well. They were on the side of health.

If I seem to go overboard on my appreciation for doctors at times, it's because I have yet to meet a doctor who is not positive for health. I've been ill many times and not *once* have I come across a doctor who isn't trying his or her best to get me back to health.

You've got to recognize that and accept it:

YOUR DOCTOR IS FOR YOU.

He's on your side.

Now the reason I know there was a change in the attitude of my three doctors is that each one of them came to my parents on the next visit and said this:

> "We've done all we know to do…but don't give up. There still may be a way."

Now I like that.

NO MATTER WHAT–THERE STILL MAY BE A WAY. DON'T GIVE UP!

Say that to yourself several times today, starting right now:

"NO MATTER WHAT–THERE STILL MAY BE A WAY. I WON'T GIVE UP!"

Every time you think of your problem—whether it's sickness or pain in some part of your body, or a broken relationship with someone you love, or a sickness in your finances—say it again:

"NO MATTER WHAT—THERE STILL MAY BE A WAY. I WON'T GIVE UP!"

Say it out loud. Say it every time you think of your problem. Get it down deep inside your attitude.

And don't be surprised if you find that other people around you begin to think it and say it, too. A good attitude rubs off on other people just like a bad attitude does.

Number Two. The second thing that happened after I got hold of my attitude and turned it around was that a man of God came to hold a meeting in a little town about 18 miles from where I grew up. He stretched a tent and started preaching that God had sent His Son Jesus to heal physically, as well as to save spiritually.

Now it just so happened that my brother Elmer and his wife were living in that little community.

My brother was not deeply religious or a practicing Christian at the time, but his wife was. And Elmer went with her to these meetings. There they saw this man lay hands on people and pray for them. Some of the people began to show evidence that they were healed, or were on the road to recovery.

Elmer was like the rest of us in the family. He didn't believe everything he saw or heard. But something stirred up in his attitude and he said, "It's worth a try."

The next thing I knew I heard a car drive up in front of our house, a step on our porch, and Elmer was in my bedroom talking to me, "Get up, Oral, and get dressed. I've come to take you to be prayed for."

I said, "Elmer, I can't get dressed. I'm too weak." (My

81

attitude was a bit down at that point.)

He said, "I'll dress you."

By that time Mama and Papa had come in asking what this was all about. When Elmer explained, my mother began to rejoice. She seemed to know that something good was going to happen. Tears ran down my father's face. They dressed me and then Elmer picked me up— mattress and all—and laid me on it in the back seat of a car he had borrowed. He had spent his last money before payday to buy enough gas to make the trip. He and Mama got in the front seat and I lay in the back seat on that mattress.

Now I want to say a word to you about what Elmer had done. There were three important things he did long before he got to our house.

WEIGH THE EVIDENCE

The first thing he did was weigh the evidence. He went to the meetings. He didn't just dismiss them or discount them. He investigated. He *looked* for evidence.

You've got to do that, too. Nobody can do it for you—although they can help. You've got to begin to think, "I'm going to look into this. It might help me."

LOOK FOR RESULTS

The second thing that Elmer did was look for *results*. He may not have believed everything he saw or heard at that meeting, but he looked at the results. He didn't dwell on the people who had nothing happen when they were prayed for. He looked at the people who were being *helped*. He let the best part of what was happening get inside his attitude.

TAKE ACTION

The third thing Elmer did was to take action. He didn't just sit at home and say to himself, "Well, *maybe* God can help Oral through this preacher." He spent his last money. He borrowed a car. He filled it with gasoline. He drove over and got me. He *did* something. He knew...

THINGS HAVE TO BE MADE TO HAPPEN

You've got to go after *your* healing too. It's not enough to just think about it...daydream about it...wonder what it might be like to get well and live in health. You've got to *do* something.

Number Three. As we rode along to that meeting—with pains shooting through my body at every bump in the road—I was listening to Elmer tell us about what he had seen and heard at the meetings. Then his voice seemed to fade away and I heard another voice deep inside me that grew louder, until it filled my head and my whole body like a roaring that gradually became more quiet. The voice said:

> "Son, I'm going to heal you
> and you're to take My healing
> power to your generation."

Nobody had to tell me that the voice was God's voice any more than they'll have to tell you when God really speaks inside you.

He may not speak to you the same as He spoke to me. He may not say the same things. He may speak to you through a sermon–something that a preacher says may just seem to leap out at you in such a big way that you don't hear anything else. You might read a verse in the Bible that will suddenly stand out. It will say something to you in a way that'll make you wonder, "Why didn't I ever see that before."

Or you might see something in nature or hear a line from a song, and it will hit you in a new way…and suddenly you'll know that it's God teaching you more about Himself and the way He does things.

You'll just know.

And what do you do when that happens?

You just accept it.

You don't start arguing about it. You don't reject it. You just take it and listen.

And I'll tell you this—after 35 years of this ministry and almost 47 years since I heard God for the first time—the more you listen for God's voice and the more you look for ways in which God might say something to you, the less you'll reject it when He does. You'll be tuned into His voice. You'll begin to learn just *how* He deals with you. And you'll know it's God.

"UNDERSTAND" AND "OBEY" ARE DIFFERENT THINGS

Right here I want to say something to you about the difference between the words *understand* and *obey*.

The Bible tells us to get understanding (Ephesians 1:17,18). We should try to understand more about God all the time. We should be reading and studying the Bible daily and listening to what anointed preachers have to say about the Bible and Jesus. We should always be learning more about God and His ways of doing things.

But the Bible *commands* us to obey.

Now there's a world of difference in being told and in being *commanded*. Let me put it this way. We are *advised* to try to improve our understanding—but we are *ordered* to obey.

Let me give you an example of this.

Suppose your house is burning and you don't know it. You're just sitting calmly in your living room. And then a neighbor comes running up to your front door and shouts at you, "Get out! Get out! Your house is on fire!"

Now you can say to yourself, "I want to try to get some more understanding about this." You can try to figure out where the fire is, what caused it, what type of fire it might be, the best ways to put it out. You can take so long trying to understand it that you burn up right along with the house.

What you have to do is *obey*! You listen to that shout and you get out of there FAST.

(And once you're outside, you might find it helpful to improve your understanding of the fire.)

That's the way it is with God. We're not commanded to figure out God. We're commanded to obey Him, and as we obey we're to look for more understanding along the way.

I DECIDED TO OBEY GOD

Lying there in the back seat of Elmer's borrowed car, I made a conscious definite decision to obey God, even though I didn't fully understand what was being said.

That's probably the best quality Oral Roberts has: obeying God regardless of anything else.

When I look back on it now, I know I was actually putting a seal on my good attitude. I had once been a fast-moving guy, hell-bent on doing my own thing. Then I had made a decision to make God a part of my life. I had *believed* that God was a good God. And that day in the back seat of that car, I made a decision to OBEY God no matter what. I was now a guy determined to do *God's* plans in *God's* way with my life.

Now that's what you might call a 180-degree turn-around—a real about-face. But that's what I chose to happen to my attitude. And it's what you can choose to happen to *your* attitude. You have to MAKE IT HAPPEN. *You* have to decide you will OBEY GOD no matter what. Nobody can do it for you.

Later my mother picked up this decision in me, and she said many times to me through the years, "Oral, stay little in your own eyes and always obey God and He'll bless the world with you."

That's the best advice my mother ever gave me. It's solid advice for you, too. OBEY GOD...and He'll bless the world with you.

Friend, there's something to this business of OBEDI-ENCE to the Living God. Are you listening? Do you have a listening heart?

Number Four. Elmer drove the car up to where the tent was stretched. They took a rocking chair into the meeting and then carried me and put me in it, with pillows to my side and back. Mama and Papa sat on either side of me. There were about 1,400 people in the tent that day, which was a really big meeting for those times in that part of the country.

I didn't hear a whole lot of what the preacher was saying. I was feverish and my lungs hurt. At times, it felt like I was being cut straight through with a knife until the pain came out underneath my shoulder blades. Mama and Papa held me up in the chair. The pillows helped some to make me more comfortable, but not much.

I told you when I started this book that there's a devil. Every negative thought you have can be traced back to him. He's real and those thoughts he tries to put in your mind are real, but you can reject them every time.

Just when you're getting into a position where something good is about to happen to you—things are moving in a good way in your life and your attitude is up—it seems something negative always starts passing through your mind. Isn't that the way it is? This has happened to me so many thousands of times that I can almost depend on it happening. But I can choose not to receive it inside me.

My body was aching. The preacher prayed for others for about two hours. And another kind of voice began to creep inside me. I had heard it before but I never tried to identify it...or think it was bad...or shut it up.

The message was something like this—"Now aren't you something? You could be home in bed with some peace and quiet. But instead you're over here in this crazy meeting where people are thinking that God heals. You really think you're going to be healed? Just because your sister said it? Just because your brother came over and made the trip to bring you here? You even thought you heard God speaking inside you. Boy, are you ever sick! You've got tuberculosis. You're going to end up in the sanatorium. You aren't going to get well. You're going to die. And not only that, but you've gone crazy believing this funny stuff."

And do you know what I did when I heard that voice?

I got mad again.

I'm sorry to say I've always had a quick temper, but I'm glad to say that when I realize I've made a mistake, I apologize for it and try to make proper corrections. But I react pretty quickly (to say the least). And I got mad.

And then I just flat out *refused* to listen. Not only do I have a quick temper, I can be real stubborn. And I got stubborn. I refused to accept that. I just labeled it a lie and shut my mind to it.

GOD IS <u>NEVER</u> NEGATIVE

That's one thing about which I'm absolutely convinced. God has *never* been negative—not one time, not in any situation, NEVER.

Anytime you hear something that's bad, discouraging, depressing, that pulls you down—that's the devil talking to you (even if it's through people or circumstances). The devil has always been a bad devil, is always a bad devil, and will always be a bad devil.

You say, "Oral Roberts, you're pretty cut and dried about that."

87

You'd better know it.

God doesn't even know how to think a negative thought. He has absolutely never had a negative attitude. There is absolutely no way that He would, could, or might cause a negative attitude in you.

God is a *good* God and He'll *always* be a *good* God.

You've got to start learning to tell the difference between the thoughts and ideas that come from God and those that come from the devil. And when you hear from God, listen to Him. OBEY HIM.

When you hear from the devil, REJECT HIM. Kick him out of your mind and life. Get mad. Get stubborn. Refuse to pay him any attention. Tell him to leave you alone and to get as far away from you as fast as he can move.

Now we've covered a lot in this chapter. I told you at the beginning that there were things that HAPPENED as soon as I had my attitude turned around.

Friend, those things were MADE TO HAPPEN. Those are things *you* can make to happen in your life. I'm going to give them to you one more time. Grab hold of them and don't let go.

> No matter what—there still may be a way.
> LOOK FOR IT. Look for evidence. Look
> for good results.
> Take action. THINGS HAVE TO BE
> MADE TO HAPPEN.
> OBEY GOD. Listen for His voice and act
> when He speaks to you.
> REFUSE TO LISTEN TO THE DEVIL.
> Ignore him cold.

You say, "Oral Roberts, that's a lot for me to do. I can't do all that."

Well, I say you can. Jesus is ready now to supply you with a full measure of help.

But you say, "You don't know me very well. I'm just not up to it. My problem is bigger than I am."

Your problem is bigger than you are, alone. But I guarantee you one thing—it isn't bigger than *you plus God*. There isn't a problem that's been thought up that's bigger than *you plus God* and your choosing to believe Him...and do things the way He does things.

And when you're hooked up to God, friend, you *can* do it. You can expect there to be a way. You can take action against the devil by obeying God. You can do it.

I know you can. Because I, a sick and dying poor young Indian boy out in the hills of Oklahoma, thought a hundred times or more that I couldn't. Then one miracle moment I chose to believe I could...and did.

And out of that came the healing...and the greatest change of my entire life. It was the moment that was a BEGINNING to the health and wholeness—and the healing ministry—I have today.

I've waited all these chapters to tell you about that moment and now we're here...

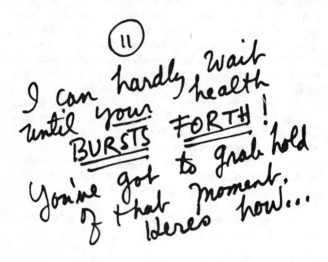

(11)

I can hardly wait until your health BURSTS FORTH! You've got to grab hold of that moment. Here's how...

The preaching part of the service finally came to an end that evening. The evangelist called for the sick to come forward. Long afterward, I was the last to be prayed for and Mama and Papa stood me up so he could pray for me.

I heard a prayer like I had never heard before. And I was ready to hear it.

Now that's a powerful combination.

When you hear the right prayer and you're READY in your attitude to hear it, things can really HAPPEN.

How was I ready to hear it?

Well, I had made up my mind that God was going to be part of my life...that God was good, that He was on my side and that I was going to obey Him. I had turned my attitude around. My attitude had become very firm and positive that God cared about my existence and was going to do something about healing me. God was really my *Source*.

Many people had planted seeds of faith in my life. And now it was time for a harvest.

My parents had planted seeds of faith in my life even when I hadn't made those seeds welcome. My sister Jewel had planted a huge seed when she said, "Oral, God is going to heal you." Elmer had planted another big seed when he went out of his way to borrow a car and drive me to the meeting. My parents had planted seeds of faith as they held me up in my chair during the meeting.

And now a preacher standing before me was planting a different but POWERFUL seed of faith—a *prayer* seed.

He was planting a kind of prayer that I had never heard before. It wasn't at all like the preacher who had visited me and said, "Son, be patient."

This man came toward me and said a prayer that went something like this:

> "You foul tormenting disease. I command you in the Name of Jesus Christ of Nazareth to loose this boy's life and lungs. Loose him and let him go free!"

I had never heard a prayer so definite or more to the point in my entire life. But I knew intuitively that this was the kind of prayer that was more apt to cause healing to burst forth in my life than some namby-pamby, milk-toast, uncertain "God, help poor Oral to be patient" prayer.

I wasn't overly smart, but a truth began to seize me and it was this:

**HEALTH IS STRONGER THAN SICKNESS.
GOD IS STRONGER THAN THE DEVIL.**

I knew I was at the right time in the right place for something good to happen to me…if I'd let it.

You know, it's a little bit frightening to think about it, but I could have lost it all at that point. I could have said, "Well, that's sure a fine prayer. Sure would be nice if it works."

But I knew I was at a DECISIVE moment. I could almost feel my attitude like a pump hammer beating staccato inside me. I believed with all I had that I WAS GOING TO GET WELL. My attitude began to believe that health was going to start breaking out inside me.

Friend, I've noticed down through the last 35 years, as I've come face–to–face with more than a million sick and hurting human beings, that the ones who have the best chance of getting their health back are those who have begun to understand that the GOOD things God put in this world are greater than the bad things that the devil has put here.

The people who have the best hope of being made whole are those who have cultivated an attitude that *God* has already put *healing powers* in their bodies and that God's health is stronger than the devil's disease.

You and I live in…

A FIERCE FIGHTING MACHINE

God made the bodies you and I live in. He made them to be fierce fighting machines. They fight every day against an onslaught of germs, viruses, and anything else that comes against them.

God also made the *chemicals* in the earth that are needed to build and to repair our bodies. The Bible says that God made our bodies out of the *dust* of the ground— and that means literally that He made them out of the earth's chemicals. This is a powerful faith-building fact for you today. And ponder this:

Not one chemical God put here is gone from the earth.

Every one of them is still in the earth. The work of scientists and medical people is to *re*–arrange the chemicals in our bodies that are out of place, or strengthen the chemicals that have been weakened, or put into us chemicals that are missing.

Don't think of their work as surgery or biology or medicine. When it comes right down to the basics, their work is to *re*-arrange the chemicals in your body according to the plan God first made.

But listen, *God also made us to be spirit*. And that has to do with your attitude, your faith in Him and His supernatural power working in you, as well as His chemicals.

And there comes a moment when your attitude and your physical being—and the chemicals in it—can come TOGETHER. They can fuse so well that you can't separate them with a paper tissue. It's a one-ness of the natural and the supernatural so that you can't tell them apart, even as your faith can't tell them apart.

You've no doubt had a moment in your life when you just felt GREAT. You were on top of the world. You just went on your way whistling, happy as could be, because everything seemed to be going GREAT. You felt good in your body so you felt good all over.

You also no doubt have had moments when your body was sick and you felt lousy clear through. Pretty soon you got a bit down and depressed about it.

Now it works in reverse, too. If you get down in your attitude—in your spirit—depressed and feeling negative and cynical about everything, you get sick a lot quicker. It's just easier to crawl into bed and shut out life and pretty soon your sickness is really holding you in its satanic grip.

And what I'm saying to you here is that you can be UP in your attitude—believing God, believing in His power of health over sickness, believing that something GOOD from Him is going to happen to you—and that this attitude of yours can make a world of difference in your health. It can bring you to that moment when health starts *bursting* forth.

Now think those things over for a few minutes. Get control of your attitude. Listen to me very carefully.

That night when Papa and Mama held me up and the man prayed for me, I heard those strong Bible-centered words and I let them fill my being.

> "Thou foul tormenting disease...I com—mand you in the Name of Jesus Christ of Nazareth to loose this boy's life and lungs. Loose him and let him go free!"

Those words seemed to whip through me like a lashing wind. And I received them. I didn't mentally fight with this man. I didn't stand there full of cynicism. I wasn't dwelling on some negative thought.

I was weak in my body—shaking like a leaf in a March wind—but inside I had made a decision. I had made a decision to receive Christ as my personal Savior, to involve Him in my whole human existence, to obey Him for the rest of my life. I had come to that miracle moment when I knew that life was rich and sweet and desirable and that God wanted me to have it.

You say, "How can I get that strong attitude working inside me?"

You just do it. Some folks will help you. Some will hinder you. But you can do it if you decide to do it. You can do almost anything if you want to do it bad enough.

GOD IS <u>NOT</u> GOING TO GIVE UP ON YOU

You say, "But how do I know that God hasn't given up on me and my health? How can I know He wants me to have my health?"

The reason I tell you firmly that God hasn't given up on you and your health is that He's already had too many

94

good chances to do that. Take me, if He had intended to give up on me, He'd have done it before that night I was prayed for. He certainly could have given up on me because I hadn't treated Him very well. And He could have given up on you, too.

But God is God and He is a *good* God, and He will *always* be a good God. He isn't going to give up on you.

You can give up on you. *You* can make a worthless thing of yourself. *You* can distort God's purposes, dash your own hopes, throw away your own dreams, and carry around sickness and disease in your body with a bitterness in your heart toward God that'll burn a hole in your will to live, like a welding torch can burn a hole through a piece of metal.

But *God isn't going to give up on you*. And, really, I don't believe *you* are going to give up on you either. If you've read this far, you're at least partially willing to believe that God is *for* you and that He wants you to have life—and have it abundantly.

When that preacher prayed and I let that prayer become a part of my attitude, so that you couldn't separate me from the attitude or the attitude from me, a *warmth* started flooding up inside me.

It didn't start in my lungs first. I felt it start in my feet, come up through my legs and my body, and engulf my whole being. I know now that this was the presence of God.

The next thing I knew, my lungs began to feel like lungs again.

You know, before I had tuberculosis, I didn't really think much about having lungs. They just worked and that's the way it was.

When I got sick, I was aware of my lungs with every breath I took. And standing there receiving healing prayer into my life, my lungs felt as if strong soft hands were settling them down, putting them back into good working order. The sharp shooting pains were leaving.

I'd grown up a stutterer. In many ways I had lived inside myself because I couldn't talk like others. If you had asked my family before that night, "Will Oral be able to say anything about it if he's healed?"—they probably would have said no.

But I tell you, God is a God of *wholeness*.

When God heals us He puts us back together so that our attitudes and our bodies are one working unit, positively believing for God's best. The same power that had welled up inside me and engulfed my lungs had also loosened my tongue.

When the evangelist said, "Son, do you have anything to say?" I found that I had a *lot* to say. It was like a dam breaking and the water rushing forth.

I want to say a little about stuttering to you.

Sometimes people who stutter are mistaken for not feeling anything or not knowing anything. That isn't true.

Some of the quickest minds I've ever known are in stuttering people. In fact, that may be part of the problem—their minds are too quick to slow down for words. Whatever the cause, people who stutter get into the habit of stuttering; and the more it becomes a habit, the more it becomes a part of the attitudes. They finally reach the place where they don't believe they *can* ever talk freely.

Based on everything I've experienced personally and with other stuttering people, I firmly believe that stuttering is about 10 percent physical and 90 percent fear. Some may say "psychological" or "attitudinal" for fear. I'm not going to argue over words. But I do know that a major breakthrough comes for most stuttering people when they can begin to *believe* that through releasing their faith to God they can learn to talk like other people. It's a time when their attitudes about themselves—and God's healing power—are turned around.

That's what happened to me that night.

The health that started BURSTING loose inside me really got turned loose. It went from my feet to my head and into every area of my being. That included every area of my attitude.

Health was BURSTING LOOSE *throughout* my being.

You say, "Oral Roberts, it all happened in just a moment of time?"

No, it didn't. But it STARTED in a moment of time.

It's right here that I've seen some people make some very serious mistakes...and some very wonderful decisions. Some people have it in their heads that a person being healed has to show some unmistakeable outward sign immediately. Otherwise, they assume that nothing is happening. That's a mistake made both about prayer and medical help. People think that if a person prays—or starts proper medication—and they don't see something dramatic happen in an instant, then nothing is happening. I've learned that's a wrong way to think.

I've prayed for some people and there was no visible sign that indicated they were being healed. And yet they would let me know weeks or months later that something HAD happened and WAS STILL HAPPENING to restore them to health and wholeness. Other people seemed to be helped immediately, but they don't go on to get much more healing after that.

Now don't get me wrong. I've seen healings that started out quick and turned out to be complete and lasting. I've seen some healings start out slow and stay slow, and very little happens. And I've seen some prayers I've prayed that didn't seem to have any effect at all.

Does it surprise you that I would say that? As a matter of fact, I've had many failures in my healing ministry. (Any doctor will tell you that he has had his or her failures, too. I don't know of any person in any profession or walk of life who has 100 percent success all the time, every time.)

But let's get back to the heart of what I'm saying to you about *your* healing and health.

Every healing has its own length of time. Some are quick. Some are slow. Some don't even appear to happen in this lifetime, but will happen through the resurrection-power of Jesus after death. (God always heals His own even if it takes the resurrection!) (We'll discuss more about that later so don't worry about it if you don't understand it right now.)

EVERY HEALING HAS ITS OWN TIME FOR COMPLETION

The matter of timing depends on lots of things. But equally true is this:

EVERY HEALING STARTS IN AN INSTANT

It may be the split second when the chemicals of your body finally start fusing into place...or when you've finally *re*-arranged the chemicals of your body through the right diet...or when you've finally balanced your checkbook...or when you've finally had that final breakthrough in communication with a relative or friend...or when your attitude and your body come together in a positive dynamic way. Or when that healing prayer meets that choice you've made to believe God with the full force of your faith. Or when a gift of healing is sent to be delivered to work in you by some servant of God.

When that instant comes for your healing to START, you have to seize it. You have to grab it and hold on. You have to believe that it's happening with every part of your being.

You have to make something happen.

EVERY BURSTING-FORTH MOMENT
OF HEALING HAS TO BE <u>SEIZED</u>.

If you don't grab hold and hang on to your moment of healing, likely you'll lose it. I almost did. And I'm going to tell you how that happened and what I did about it so you don't ever have to make my mistake...

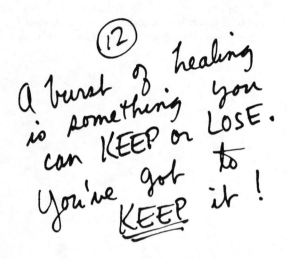

(12)

A burst of healing is something you can KEEP or LOSE. You've got to KEEP it!

Did you know that you can lose a healing? That you can squelch it after it bursts forth?

You can.

I'm determined you aren't going to do that. You've got to read this chapter carefully.

Following the start of my healing that night, we all got back in the car and drove home.

It sure was nice not to have to lie down on the mattress in the back seat. I could sit up and share in the conversation about the good thing that had begun in me.

It never occurred to me that I might have a relapse. It just never *dawned* on me that the feeling that had flooded through me might go away.

That didn't mean that I had not truly experienced the start of my healing. I had. It was the most thrilling moment of my life to that point. It was *real*. But in all of my good feeling, I just assumed that the bursting-forth time would go on and on.

I am absolutely certain there is a BURSTING-FORTH time for healing. My health began to burst forth inside me in an instant. I could feel it. I knew it was happening.

You may not feel it. You may not experience this bursting-forth time in the same way that I did. But in your being healed, it's there whether you feel it or not, or even whether you are aware of it or not. That is something you can absolutely depend upon. There is a point spiritually or medically or both when health starts becoming stronger than disease. It's the moment of reversal—when disease takes a U-turn and you begin to get better instead of worse.

You say, "Oral Roberts, I'm apparently a quieter person than you are. My feelings don't run as deep as yours. Things happen to me more gently. Suppose I don't feel my health bursting forth like you did?"

Well, first I accept you as you are because I believe God does. If you're one of those slow-fused persons, so be it.

Second, even if the burst of health is so small—even if it's to the point where it's almost unidentifiable—I want to assure you that it *does* take place and you're to look for it to take place.

It's like a seed you plant. There's a time when the seed just lies there in the ground. But you'd be inspired if you were able to see it at a certain time—just at the point when it begins to crack open and the green shoot BURSTS out. You'd understand better what I'm trying to say to you.

I've gone down to the science department at Oral Roberts University and seen this happen through a microscope and I'm absolutely convinced that there is a BURSTING-FORTH TIME for a seed to change its nature so it can become a plant and grow and produce fruit. It's a principle, a fundamental basic law of God. It's true for a seed and it's true in all areas of life.

I'm equally convinced that there is a time when you and I start meeting the conditions of God's health system for us on this earth...a time for us to get our attitudes moving in the right direction...a time when the conditions are right for your health to start BURSTING forth. Don't be concerned *how* it happens. Just look for it to happen.

And you must grab hold of that moment and CONTINUE to go in an upward direction. My favorite way of saying it is: Expect a Miracle!

It never occurred to me in that night my healing began that I hadn't truly changed *all* of my attitude toward being a healthy person, and that I didn't really know I would have to seek to make the rest of my health *continue* to happen.

Let me tell you what happened.

During the next several days after the healing meeting, I was almost like any other person. I began to act well. I didn't hemorrhage again. I didn't have those awful spells of coughing. I didn't experience the nightly bed sweats.

My appetite returned. I was able to walk around. The signs of being a normal human being were reappearing.

But you see, I had judged it wrong. I had misunderstood my healing. A miracle was not something I understood or had ever expected. And I didn't know how to handle it.

Why didn't I know how to handle it?

Well, I hadn't been grounded *personally* in the Word of God, the Bible. Most of what I had learned about the Bible was second-hand or third-hand. I took things directly—but mostly indirectly—from my parents and the preachers in the church I grew up in. I didn't know about the *way* Jesus healed people. (In other words, I hadn't learned about the way God does things.)

How did Jesus heal people?

He said, "Be thou made *whole*," or, "Thy faith hath made thee whole," or, "Take up thy bed and walk."

The basic flaw in my understanding about healing was that God deals in *whole-person healing*, not just disease-healing.

JESUS WANTS TO HEAL THE WHOLE OF YOU

You say, "Oral Roberts, what are you trying to tell me?"

I'm saying that God sees you as a *whole*. You may think your problem is some disease and that it's just physical...or just a problem in a relationship...or just a financial problem...or just a spiritual problem. That's not the entire truth of the matter. Whatever the *main* problem appears to be, it becomes a problem in *every* area of your life. And you don't solve the *entire* problem when you solve just one part of it.

In my life, my *body* had experienced a bursting-forth of healing. But my attitude was still sick. I was still thinking and feeling and believing like a *sick* person. I, myself, had not been made *whole*.

I want to say something else to you, too, about this matter of being *whole*.

At one time in my life, I thought of sickness as your *eye* being sick, or your *heart* being sick, or your *lungs* being sick.

When I've been in hospitals, I've heard doctors and nurses make statements like "the eye in Room 224," or, "the heart in Room 294."

At first, I didn't know what they meant, except to think they had some part of the body up there that had been separated from a person. Later I learned that they had just fallen into the bad habit of *not* saying, "I have a pa-

103

tient up in this room with a bad eye"—or foot, or heart, or whatever the problem was.

I don't like that. I didn't like it then and I don't like it now. I don't think we have any right to talk about a human being in that way. God didn't create us a foot plus a heart plus an eye. He created us as human beings—spirit, mind, body, emotions, relationships, material needs. (Read I Corinthians 12:12-20.)

You've got a body...but you're more than physical.

You've got a mind...but you're more than mental.

You've got emotions...but you're more than emotions.

You are a spiritual being who has a body, and a mind, and a set of emotions, and an attitude, and material goods and finances. God sees you as a *whole*.

That's one thing we're really trying to drastically change at the City of Faith Medical and Research Center. And we're starting to have a lot of success with it. People coming to the City of Faith are telling us that they feel cared for *"as a number ONE person"* when they're under our care. We are making a wholehearted and well-planned effort to treat medically and pray spiritually for people as a *whole*.

You've got to see yourself as a *whole*, too, so that you can really understand this:

> NO MATTER what's wrong with you...it's part of a whole. God wants you *whole* with every part of your life working.

And when you come to the City of Faith as a patient, come in that attitude. Work at it, because God does and we do, too.

HOW YOU CAN BE <u>MADE</u> WHOLE

I want you to notice one more thing in what Jesus said to people when He healed them.

He often said, "Be thou *made* whole." Whole-person

104

healing is both a beginning act and a continuing process that never stops.

I'm going to say that again so you can try to get it deep within you:

> WHOLE-person healing is a
> BEGINNING ACT
> and
> a CONTINUING <u>PROCESS</u>.

It's two things. It's a start. And it's an on-going process, day by day.

If you stop either one of those two things, the entire healing process stops. If you have a bursting-forth moment, you can destroy it if you don't continue on.

Friend, you've got to be *made* whole. And you've heard me say it before, and I'm going to say it again...

THINGS HAVE TO BE <u>MADE</u> TO HAPPEN

You have to go after wholeness. It doesn't just happen automatically. But I didn't know that the night my healing began.

After a few days of feeling on top of the world, the shine began to rub off. My strength began to ebb. The burst of health I had experienced just seemed to get weaker and weaker.

Mama came around the corner of the house one day and she found me sitting with my back up against the wall. She had a gift of understanding and she realized immediately that I was discouraged.

She said, "Oral, you think you weren't really healed, don't you?"

Well, Mama," I said. "Why do I still feel so weak? Why don't I feel the way I did that night—strong enough to do anything?"

She said, "Oral, you've been sick a long time. You've been in bed for over five months. The tuberculosis, no

105

doubt, had taken root in you long before they brought you home. Now God has begun to heal you. You're on the right path to getting well. But you've got to remember a couple of things."

"Like what, Mama?"

"First, you've got to remember how you felt when you received the healing prayer."

"You mean the burst of health that just seemed to explode in me?"

"Yes. Don't you ever think that wasn't real or that it didn't happen. Remember the beginning of your healing and expect it to continue."

"Well, Mama, why do I have to lie down some during each day? Why don't I have enough strength to stay up all day and be normal again?"

"Oral, there's one thing I'm going to tell you to do, and I speak in the Name of the Lord. It's perfectly OK for you to lie down some during the day. In fact, you should do that while you're getting your strength back. But when you lie down, DON'T take off your clothes and get into your pajamas, and crawl under the covers."

"What am I supposed to do then?"

She said, "Oral, if you have to lie down for 20 or 30 minutes—or even for a couple of hours—keep your clothes on and lie down across the top of the bed. Don't get under the covers until it's bedtime at night."

"Well, what will that accomplish—my lying down with my clothes on instead of getting into my pajamas in bed?"

"It will help your attitude. If you take off your clothes and crawl back into bed during the day, you may be actually causing your attitude to say, 'I have had no beginning of a healing. I'm not going to get well. I'll be sick the rest of my life and this will be my end.' That's what you'll be learning as an attitude.

"But when you stay on top of your bed with your everyday clothes on, it helps your attitude to say, 'I'm in the

KEEP YOUR HEALING

process of being healed. My own faith is still working. My family is believing with me and for me. The doctors are still helping me. I'm getting well!' "

"What happens if I don't do that, Mama? What happens if I just crawl back into bed?"

"Well, Oral, pretty soon the symptoms of that disease will begin to fasten themselves on you again. Remember, you took the medicines the doctors gave you because you had faith. You received healing prayers because you had faith. You are *still* operating in faith at all times for your health. It takes FAITH, Oral, to make your healing *continue* to happen. It's in your attitude."

My mother, as I've told you, was part Indian. And when Mama had said all she came to say, she abruptly turned and walked away. That was it. I could take it or leave it. She had come to help me. But she couldn't make me do it and she *wouldn't* make me do it. She had told me how to change my attitude and get into an attitude of health-receiving, health-expectancy, and health-goals. Not just healing, but *whole health*.

The bottom line was that I was going to have to help MAKE IT HAPPEN by changing my own attitude and doing what she had said.

Are you listening?

Do you have a listening heart?

I obeyed what Mama said...literally. I took naps and rested. But I never crawled back into bed in the middle of the day. It took almost a year for my healing to become *health*. Did you hear what I said?

A HEALING MUST BECOME HEALTH

It took a year for the burst of healing to grow and produce whole-person *health* in my life. It took a year for my lungs to become completely *strong* and *whole*. It took a year for my tongue to be *free* of stuttering.

And I don't want you to think that year was easy. It was

107

one of the most difficult years of my life.

You see, I had become a half-spoiled brat when I was sick. Sick people aren't usually the easiest folks to get along with, and even when they are in the process of getting well they can be pretty difficult.

In the days when I had been crawling back into bed during the middle of the day, I had become a pain in the neck to my family. I wanted the same special attention that I had known before. They had waited on me hand and foot. The doctors had come often. I had liked that. It was hard for me to give up those things.

But I had to do it. I HAD TO MAKE MY HEALING TURN INTO HEALTH. I had to start doing things for myself and to stand on my own.

I had to start seeing myself as a *well* person instead of as a sick person. I have a friend whose wife decided one day to give up and go to bed. She wasn't sick. She was elderly and just wanted someone to take care of her. She just gave up. That woman never got up again. She was in that bed for years until she died. She saw herself as sick and not well. Her attitude spelled death.

God has a better way for *you*. And I'm excited to tell you about it and to help you learn how to use a point of contact to help you release your faith...to get your faith going up and out of you to God instead of just going on. The point of contact is going to be powerful for you.

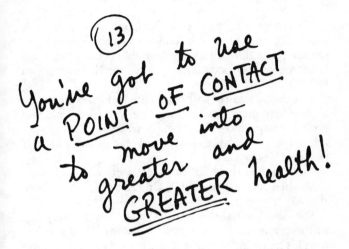

13

You've got to use a POINT OF CONTACT to move into greater and GREATER health!

When I began praying for the sick (which I continue to do this very day, including praying for people in the letters I write to them), I soon learned that getting people to DO SOMETHING is actually a Point of Contact.

I've used a Point of Contact practically every day of my life for more than 35 years, both with myself and with other people. I know that people who have used the Point of Contact have found that it works.

That's why I want to share it with you. The Point of Contact has a proven track record. It can work in your life…if you work it.

Note that last line again…*if you work it*. A Point of Contact is something *you* do, and when *you* do it, it causes *your* faith to come up out of *your* heart and go to God.

I remember people used to tell me, "Oral Roberts, I've got all the faith in the world and I'm still not well."

I would reply, "That's your trouble. You still have the faith."

It's not enough to HAVE faith any more than it is enough to have money or food or clothing. You have to release these things and get them into action. You have to *use* money, *eat* food, *wear* clothing, and that means you DO SOMETHING.

You can be a miser with your faith just like you can be a miser with money or anything else. I've read—and you probably have, too—about people who have died of starvation even though they had money stashed away in their homes to buy food.

Isn't it awful to have faith and not use it?

Maybe you say to me, "But, Oral Roberts, I don't have any faith to use."

The fact is, you do have faith. You do use it, every day and every hour. Faith is right believing. Said another way, it's believing the right things about God. It is believing that God is God—God is a *good* God and He will always be a good God. It's also believing that God always meets you at the point of your need—at each step you take.

The Bible says that every person has a MEASURE of faith (Romans 12:3). However much faith you have is how much faith you NEED to make things happen in your life. God has put the faith in you but you are to release it back to Him. It's a double-release. You release your faith to Him, He releases His power to you.

How do you get the lights on in your house? Why do you turn on the light switch? That switch is connected to the power plant. The electricity is always there. But it's only released into your house when you turn on the switch.

The Point of Contact is the same principle. God is always ON, friend. He is always there ready to put things into motion to meet your needs. When you release your faith, you put God's blessings of life more abundant into motion.

The first time I knew about a Point of Contact was when I was praying for two sisters in 1947. One of them, Irma, had never really recovered her full *healing* from tuberculosis so she could be in *health*.

When I reached out to touch Irma and to pray for her, I became aware of a warmth or heat in my right hand. It engulfed my entire being softly—but it was so sharply concentrated in my right hand that I was most aware of it there. When I touched Irma, it felt like something was going out of me.

"Oral," she said, "What did you do to me?"

I said, "Irma, I prayed for you."

She said, "But there was this warmth that came through your hand and surged through my body. And it's doing it right now. I'm being healed."

"Irma," I said, "this is new to me. As far as I can tell, it is a Point of Contact."

I don't know where those words came from. Maybe I'd read them or heard them. But that was the first time they became personal property to me—a phrase that I could use with understanding about how to release my faith to help people get in touch with God.

Irma began to get into health that day, and she went on to be completely cured.

Later, I learned through many experiences that this warmth in my right hand was like a signal to me. It was something that God had given to me, Oral Roberts, to recognize and to use as a Point of Contact. When I felt that warmth in my hand, I knew it was time to release my faith fully to God and to touch people. It was a signal that

111

I was to DO SOMETHING and that things were being set in motion. (This is not the only Point of Contact I use.)

Just recently Evelyn had lost the feeling on one side of her head. It was the result of a traffic accident that we'd had—and although she was up and moving about and getting back her energy, this was giving her a bad headache.

I reached out my hand to pray for her, and when I did, the power of God shot through my arm and hand and into her head all the way down through her body. The feeling returned, and Evelyn went about her day's work, normal again. My hand was her Point of Contact. She used it to release her faith to God.

That feeling in my hand—that warm sensation of electric-like power—is a signal, a Point of Contact, and it has been for 35 years.

After the first time I felt this, I made a study of the Point of Contact in the entire Bible. I saw that many people had used different types of methods as a Point of Contact.

The New Testament alone has a number of examples about how people used this method.

Jesus *touched* people with His hands. He put His *fingers* in a man's ears. He put some *moist clay* on a blind man's eyes. He *spoke* to people. The *sound* of His voice was a Point of Contact with them. He let one woman *touch the hem of His clothing* and she received her healing. These were specific things. They were very real and practical actions that were Points of Contact between Jesus and the persons who needed healing.

In the book of Acts in the New Testament, we read that the *shadow* of Peter's body fell upon the sick. That shadow became a Point of Contact and people were healed and delivered (Acts 5:15).

In Acts 19:11, 12, *handkerchiefs* were taken from Paul and laid upon the sick and they were healed. The hand-

112

kerchiefs became a Point of Contact to help the sick release their faith to God.

Jesus said in Luke 5:31, "They that are sick need a
physician."

Your *visit* to a doctor may be your Point of Contact. The
Point of Contact may come through the *prescription* that
the doctor writes, or through *surgery*, or through some
other medical treatment. That doctor is doing something
in a specific, practical way to help you. Take it and use
it as a Point of Contact for releasing your faith up to God
Who is the Source of all healing.

I want to really drive it home to you—

I never have, don't now, and never expect to make a
major difference between supernatural and natural healing. Jesus told me that we can't put even a piece of tissue
paper between His natural and supernatural power. He
made it all. He combined them to work together—as a
whole. We human beings have separated God's power
into different categories. And we've got to stop it.

The practical down-to-earth things that you can use as
a Point of Contact are just as supernatural as they are natural. They are just as natural as they are supernatural.
The medicines that a doctor uses come out of God's earth,
"The earth is the Lord's and the fulness thereof" (Psalm
24:1), and are in a sense as supernatural as they are natural. The prayer we use is both natural and supernatural.
As a natural human being turned on to God and called to
pray for the sick, I seek to go from the natural to the
supernatural—but to the same Source: God. And in medical care this is what we are developing at the City of Faith
here in Tulsa. To get God's natural and supernatural together is what He is showing us to do for you—and as a
merger to permeate the whole healing process for mankind.

113

ACTIVATE YOUR ATTITUDE
YOUR ATTITUDE IS IN YOUR RIGHT HAND

I've told you how I often feel a warmth in my hand when I pray for people and how that is one of *my* Points of Contact. Other Points of Contact I use are my preaching, a word of knowledge, praying in the Spirit, giving a specific scripture, or having a person touch himself or touch someone else. I'm convinced of this—your attitude can be placed in a Point of Contact so you can release it to God. It may very definitely become your attitude—an attitude to DO SOMETHING.

You say, "What are you trying to tell me, Oral Roberts? What do you mean by my attitude being in my right hand?"

I mean this—the term *right hand* has always been used to mean your *powerful* hand. It also means symbol of power. So as I use the term think of it for yourself in that way. In other words...

> you can place your attitude in your powerful hand and do something with it. YOU CAN MAKE SOMETHING HAPPEN. You can *take charge*.

I'm going to give you some examples so you can get this *working* in your life for your healing and health in every area of need.

(14)

You must get your attitude into YOUR hand and turn it into a POINT OF CONTACT.

Recently, I preached to our more than 4,000 students at Oral Roberts University about the placing of their attitudes into their hands.

One of the students came up to me afterwards and said, "But *how* do I do that? How can I get my attitude into *my* hand?"

That's what I want to share with you in this chapter. This is a very practical chapter. It's going to hit close to home. Are you listening? Do you have a listening heart?

HOW TO GET YOUR ATTITUDE INTO YOUR HAND

Has the doctor prescribed some medicine for you to

take?

Then hold that medicine in your *hand* a moment. Look at it. Your attitude will determine what you do with it. Are you going to take it or just look at it? You have to put your *hand* to your mouth in order to take it. When you do that, you've put your attitude in your hand and done something with it.

Is something wrong in your body?

Have you seen a physician about it?

You might say to me, "I'm scared to see a doctor."

Many people are. You aren't alone. But that doesn't make it OK to avoid seeing a doctor. *You have to see a doctor and establish a relationship.*

God has allowed that doctor to be trained as a way of helping you. That doctor is one of God's instruments— whether he always acknowledges it or not—and you must not cut yourself off from one of the ways that God may choose to heal you. I work at my relationship with my personal physician, and with those whose ministry gift is prayer. I need and want both. I especially appreciate it when my doctor also prays for me. (More doctors are courageously doing this today.)

Now your attitude is going to be put into your hand. Pick up your telephone. It's in your hand. What are you going to do with it? Are you going to hang it back up? Or are you going to dial that doctor and make an appointment and keep it and get yourself on the road to health? Put your attitude in your hand and do something with it—dial that doctor today.

If you need to make an appointment at the City of Faith, then dial the City of Faith *918-493-1000.*

I've put that number on a separate page so you can find it easier if you ever need it.

And after you've called your physician, pick up that phone again and call the Abundant Life Prayer Group here in Tulsa. These are dedicated men and women who are on duty 24 hours a day in the Prayer Tower at the center of the Oral Roberts University campus. They can *really* pray for you. Their number is *918-492-7777*. Get the best of prayer moving in your direction! DO ALL YOU CAN DO. Don't shortchange yourself or cut off ANY of God's ways of helping you.

Are you overweight and in need of losing some weight so you'll really be able to get into complete health? At your next meal, hold your fork out in front of you. It's in your *hand*. What are you going to do with it? Your attitude has been placed in your hand. Are you going to put it back down and realize you've had enough for this meal? Or are you going to eat that forkful of food even when you don't need it?

Are you listening?

Do you have a listening heart?

The Bible mentions many times where people "laid their *hands* on the sick" and they recovered. (You read the book of Acts with *hands* in mind and you'll see it again and again.)

What does this mean?

It means that they put their attitudes in their hands and then they released their attitudes to DO SOMETHING. They prayed and touched the people with their *hands*.

On my television programs, I always offer healing prayer, then say:

> "Let's pray. Touch someone in the room with you, or if you are alone, touch yourself."

I've even suggested to people that they place their hands on a radio or on the television as I pray. Now some folks have thought that was pretty silly. How could anyone get well by touching a television set? But they didn't understand that it had nothing to do with the television set at all. It is a Point of Contact—something specific to do and it was a way of placing their attitudes in their hands. It is a way to use their attitudes to DO SOMETHING to MAKE THINGS HAPPEN. To let their faith go up to God.

YOU'VE GOT TO FIND YOUR POINT OF CONTACT

That's the reason I've been telling you all these things.

You've got to get your attitude into your hand and do something with it.

One way that I know—and it's a way that has worked for many people for many years—is to write a letter.

Get that pen in your *hand*. You have your attitude in your hand. You can use it to WRITE A LETTER and then when you MAIL THAT LETTER you are releasing your faith to God. It's something specific and practical that you DO with your hand or some other means.

A letter between me and another person is often the most powerful thing between us to release our faith. Exchanging letters is a powerful Point of Contact.

I love to preach the Gospel, to pray for the sick, to build things for God and to help other people. I love to try to help people to stand taller in their faith and love. I write books like the one you're reading and send them around the world to people who ask for them to help get their needs met. I publish magazines and teach classes and speak and pray on television programs and preach at other gatherings as time permits.

But, friend, the most powerful thing I do—and the thing that I can do best to help *you*—is to answer your letter to me in which you tell me like it is with you.

A LETTER TO ME IS A POINT OF CONTACT

Just this week I read a letter I received from a mother who lives in a small town. I asked her if I could share a part of her letter with you and she agreed.

IN TIMES OF CRISIS...

The Abundant Life Prayer Group is located in the Prayer Tower at the center of the Oral Roberts University campus.

Get your attitude firmly into your powerful hand. When you are in trouble, get the telephone receiver in your hand and call the ABUNDANT LIFE PRAYER GROUP in Tulsa, Oklahoma, for prayer...

Dial
918 . 492-7777

Tear out this page and keep it handy

Get ALL of God's power to work on your case!

City of Faith Medical and Research Center in Tulsa, Oklahoma

When you are in need of whole-person health care from one of our Christian physicians, call ...

CITY OF FAITH MEDICAL AND RESEARCH CENTER
918 · 493-1000

She wrote:

> Dear Brother Roberts,
> I've discovered one thing in writing to you on a regular basis. Every time I sit down to write, I know you will keep my letter in confidence so I have this good feeling that I can say anything. My whole being opens up. I just write what I feel. And that always makes me start feeling better.
> Then when I seal the letter, put a stamp on it, and mail it, I can actually feel my faith going up to God.

(That's *right*! Her letter is a Point of Contact. That woman has her attitude in her powerful hand. She's doing something with it. She's releasing her faith up to God. She's MAKING SOMETHING HAPPEN. She's setting into motion the things that need to HAPPEN for God to work in her life.)

> I know it takes a few days to get a letter to you. But while that letter is in the mail, I always have this feeling that something has already started to happen. I've done what I can to MAKE THINGS HAPPEN. I've used a Point of Contact and my faith is released.
> And then when I get your letter back, open it, and start reading it, it's like we're sitting down face-to-face. You write like you talk and you talk like you write. Pretty soon you've said something that touches me and I know that the Lord has guided you to give me some specific things to do to help me use my faith in other ways. Several times my healing has begun even be-

121

fore I finish reading your letter.

(I've heard that same thing so often from other people that it is really encouraging. I believe them because they are telling me about a principle that's in the Bible. *It's a life principle*. She's using both her letter and my letter as Points of Contact. She's getting her attitude into her hand and doing something with it.)

> I hope this doesn't offend you, but sometimes I don't get what I need from the first reading of your letter.

(She didn't know she wasn't the first person who had told me that.)

> I've read some of your letters over and over until I've nearly worn them out. It took that long for it to sink in what God was trying to say to me through you. But that's the beautiful part about a letter. I can read it over and over. I always have it.
>
> You've taught me that writing a letter is one of the most important things I'll ever do, especially when I do it on a regular basis.
>
> And I want you to know, I like one thing about you. When I write you, you'll write me back. I *look* for your letter.

That's important. When you are *looking* for something, you're in a better condition to receive it and get your faith going up to God.

Now her letter isn't all that unusual. I get lots of letters like that because letter-writing between my partners and me is precious. It works. It is a Point of Contact. I enjoy receiving letters for my prayers and I enjoy answering them.

The Bible, especially the New Testament, is a record of *letters* from men and women of God. They wrote under divine inspiration to people like you and me to tell us about God and how God wants us to live. God has honored the letter-writing method.

Some people have asked me, "Oral Roberts, do you write your own letters?"

I might as well deal with that right here. The answer is yes.

Long ago I developed a Bible-based letter-writing technique. The second book of Corinthians begins by saying that Paul is writing the letter. And then it says "and Timothy." Apparently, God was giving the inspired words to Paul, who was giving them to Timothy to transcribe them and write them down and mail them to the church. But the people who got the letter knew it was from Paul. And it didn't matter if Timothy and others helped him to get the letter written and delivered.

Yes, I write the words in my own letters. No one can say it like I feel it from God. But if I didn't have some trusted people to help me get that letter typed and mailed to you, you would never get it from me. I am studying all the time how to do this better, but the bottom line is this:

Our letter is a letter between *you* and *me*. And it is a Powerful Point of Contact for both of us to release our faith to God for His answer. I frankly say that I believe my letter-writing service is one of the most effective ways God used to help you get healing and come into health— spiritually, physically, financially, and with members of your family. My practice is not to write until a person first writes to me. This usually indicates a need. Then I can deal with that need in a specific way. I want to answer your letters on a *regular* basis. I commit to you that I will give you my best prayer and replies on a regular basis. This can be one of the most life-inspiring parts of our Blessing-Pact Partnership with God.

Are you listening?

Do you have a listening heart?

You need a Point of Contact for releasing your faith. It needs to be something practical, something specific.

AGAIN, WHAT IS A POINT OF CONTACT?

A Point of Contact is something you do...and *when* you do it you cause your faith to go up out of your heart TO God. It's not enough to have faith. Your faith is in you to be turned loose—to be sent to God, your Savior and Source.

When you get to a place in life where you need healing and health in any way—in your spirit, your body, your emotions, your finances, your relationships, your entire attitude—you START getting God's answer by dealing directly with God. You start the way He said—with your faith. "The righteous shall live by faith" (Romans 1:17). Faith and "to live" go hand in hand.

As a faith man, one who spends my life on making my faith work, and in helping you make your faith work, I use a Point of Contact. I use different ones, depending on the circumstances or how I am led.

Again, I tell you that using your Point of Contact is in your *attitude*, which I keep reminding you is, symbolically, in your right hand.

Therefore, here's what I want you to do:

First, lay this page on your body as a Point of Contact and say to your faith: "Faith, go up to God! Faith, go up to God!"

Say this several times until you are sensing you are taking hold of your inner being and it's becoming your very attitude itself. Then it will be real and your faith will go up to God and something GOOD will begin to form and loom ahead for you.

Second, feel free to pick up a pen and write me a letter,

however short. Talk to me. Get something off your heart. I will hold it in confidence and answer you back.

Third, take your strong hand (right or left) and stretch it forth as if you are literally taking your attitude in it. Then say, "Thank You, God, that I now have my attitude in my strong hand. And I'm focusing it on You as my Source, my Source of total supply. And, God, I expect a miracle!"

Do any or all of these things. Get things happening. MOVE!

(15)

You've got to use the Name of Jesus. It's the most powerful tool you have.

Now I'm going to give you one portion of scripture that can really change your thinking about sickness and disease. It can help you make one giant leap on your way to *whole* health.

Are you ready for it? Are you listening?

It's in Philippians 2:5-11:

"Let this mind be in you, which was also in Christ Jesus: who, being in the form of God, thought it not robbery to be equal with God: but made himself of no reputation, and took upon him the form of a servant, and was made in the likeness of men: and being found in fashion as a man, he humbled himself, and became obedient

126

unto death, even the death of the cross.

Wherefore God also hath <u>highly</u> <u>exalted</u> <u>him</u>, and given him <u>a name</u> <u>which</u> <u>is</u> <u>above</u> <u>every</u> name: <u>that</u> <u>at</u> <u>the name</u> <u>of</u> Jesus <u>every</u> <u>knee</u> <u>should</u> <u>bow</u>, of things in heaven, and things in earth, and things under the earth; and that every tongue should confess that Jesus Christ is Lord, to the glory of God the Father."

Note that underlined part. That's pretty simple to understand. The name of Jesus is greater than any name of anything on the earth.

But you say, "What does that have to do with my health?"

Well, if you're sick or have a *dis*-ease, there is a name attached to that ailment. It might be a name like "arthritis"...or "diabetes"...or "headache"...or "high blood pressure"...or "cancer." It could be one of any number of other names. The name sums up everything that is wrong with your eye, or ear, or shoulder, or lung, or stomach, or other part of you.

Now what I'm about to say to you is something that has really helped me, continues to help me, and is causing hundreds of thousands of people to get help. Do you have a listening heart?

First, think of the name of the *dis*-ease or sickness that is troubling you. (You've noticed, haven't you, how I keep saying *dis*-ease. *Dis*-ease is a lack of ease. It's a lack of harmony. It may be in your relationships, or your finances, or your body. You are out-of-ease.)

Think of the name of what's bothering you and then...

Second, think of the Name of JESUS. See it plainly in your mind. Place it above the name of the *dis*-ease.

In your mind it might look like this (and I'm only using arthritis as an example):

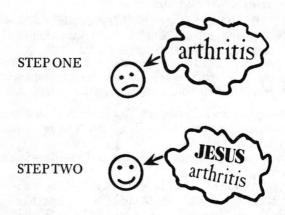

And third, imagine in your mind that the Name of JESUS becomes larger and larger so that it just wipes out the name of arthritis, or whatever *your dis*-ease or ailment is.

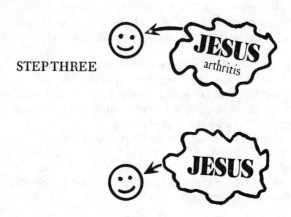

You say, "Oral Roberts, what are you trying to get me

to do here?"

I'm trying to get you to see that the name of any *dis*-ease that you may have is not nearly as strong or powerful as the Name of JESUS in your life. His name is greater than any other word you can think of. He is above...more powerful...with all authority to wipe that *dis*-ease away.

Now I don't just say it's so. The Bible says it. Read it again.

> "God hath <u>highly</u> exalted him, and <u>given him a name</u> <u>which</u> <u>is</u> <u>above</u> <u>every</u> <u>name</u>..."(Philippians 2:9, 10).

And catch the next phrase:

> "That at the *name of Jesus* every knee should bow."

That means *everything*. Every illness. Every worry or trouble.

You say, "How does this all relate to my healing and health?"

It relates like a glove on a hand.

Let me remind you briefly of something I said in the beginning of this book about the worst mistake I ever made in my life. It was this: I failed to come to terms with the fact of all facts. That fact is that God is a *good* God. I hadn't dealt GOD into my life. I didn't have the Name of JESUS in my life. I had refused to make Him a part of my daily existence.

What I did have in my life was the name of "tuberculosis." It was knocking me flat and keeping me bedfast. I would have *died* with the name of tuberculosis in me.

Once I had the Name of JESUS in me...once I had accepted Him as my personal Savior and the Source of my healing...that Name was also in there alongside tuberculosis. I had two names in me: JESUS and tuberculosis. And when I put the Name of JESUS up over tuberculosis...and began to realize and believe that JESUS was stronger and more powerful than the name of tuberculosis...well, the Name of JESUS wiped out the name of tuberculosis. It put it on the run, and out of my life forever.

That isn't to say that the name of tuberculosis wasn't serious. The papers had been signed for me to be taken to the state sanatorium. It was not only serious, it was stubborn and growing. And I went almost to the end of my life at age 17 before I got the Name of JESUS into me so it could do something to the name of tuberculosis.

You see, I had an attitude that the name of tuberculosis was greater than anything else in the universe. It had a grip on me and was killing me. I thought it was the most powerful thing ever known.

And then I got the truth working inside me that JESUS was *more powerful* than tuberculosis. JESUS was in me, too. JESUS—and all of the perfect health He held in His hand—was more powerful than any disease or illness.

And that's when my health began to burst forth.

Can you imagine how much better things would have been for me if I could have gotten that truth working in my life the *first* month I had tuberculosis...instead of waiting until after the fifth month? It probably wouldn't have taken a whole year for me to get back my strength. I wouldn't have been in such agony in my mind.

But it didn't happen that way. And it didn't happen because I DIDN'T MAKE IT HAPPEN. I didn't allow JESUS to be greater in me than anything else.

I want to give you another scripture:

> "Hitherto have ye asked nothing in my name: ask, and ye shall receive, that your joy may be full" (John 16:24).

JESUS' name has in it all power of heaven and earth. It can and *will* break the devil's grip. It will loose you from bondage. It will set you free from sin. It will free you from *dis*-eases and sicknesses. It is greater than any problem you have.

For many years I have said this on our television programs, and Richard and the singers sing it often:

> "Greater is He who is in you than he that is in the world."

That's a direct quote from the Bible (I John 4:4). It means just what we've been talking about:

> GREATER IS JESUS in you than any disease that is from the devil in this world.

Get the truth of this alive and stirred up in you:

> GOD IS GREATER THAN THE DEVIL...
> HEALTH IS GREATER THAN DISEASE...
> THE NAME OF JESUS IS GREATER
> THAN ANY NAME OF ANYTHING
> ON THE FACE OF THIS EARTH!

Friend, I didn't know a fraction of that when I had tuberculosis. I'm still learning more about it. But I know that had my family been millionaires, they would have given every dollar they had for the powerful information that is now in your hands. It was the key to my health. And after all, what are you without health? What was Oral Roberts without health? Can you put a dollar value on any person's life? Can you put monetary value on health?

Suppose you lost ten dollars and that was all the money you had. You didn't have any money to buy groceries to feed your family for even one meal. (Having been in that particular place in my life and with my family several times, I know how it feels.)

But suppose at the same time there was somebody who cared for you, and they came up to you and said, "Here's a hundred dollar bill. Take it. Use it. It's yours."

I know what you'd do. Once you got over the shock of it, you'd smile great big and say, "Thank YOU" and start feeling better all over. You'd throw your shoulders back, take a deep breath, and move forward in your life to get the things you needed.

Well, that's the same thing I'm talking about. You've got to grasp what total health is. You've got to identify by *name* what is pulling you away from total health. And then you've got to realize that the Name of JESUS is above it...is greater...is more powerful than anything that is dragging you down.

YOU MUST PUT THE NAME OF JESUS ABOVE YOUR PROBLEM.

You've got a sickness or a *dis*-ease. It has a name. It's either wearing you down or destroying you and it's about to take you out. There's one thing sure about it, you're not enjoying it. And you think about it many times a day. You might be thinking about it almost constantly.

You probably say to yourself or to someone else, "That pain in my back is killing me." You have back pain. It's a name. Or, "My asthma is sure bothering me today." You have asthma. It's a name.

At the same time, if you have the Name of JESUS in your life, you have a Name in you right alongside what is bothering you. It's up to you...NOW...TODAY...to put the Name of JESUS ABOVE that sickness or *dis*-ease.

You can do it. Only you can do it.

You say, "But Oral Roberts, what if Jesus doesn't choose to place His Name directly above my sickness or *dis*-ease so it can be wiped out?

You're asking the wrong question.

To get right answers you've got to ask right questions.

I'm going to give you some examples of right and wrong questions. Let them sink into you.

These are WRONG questions: "What have I done to

deserve this?" "Why doesn't God heal me?" "If God is as good as Oral Roberts says He is, why doesn't Jesus just automatically fix me up from head to toe?"

Now let me give you an example of the *right* kinds of questions:

RIGHT QUESTION   "There's enough evidence all around me that God is God, He is good, so why don't I recognize God and his goodness?"

RIGHT QUESTION   "There's a group of people I know who are a praying group and who can get a prayer through to God on my behalf, so why don't I take time to start developing my spiritual life, associate with them, and start learning how to join my prayers with theirs and say to my faith, 'Go up to God. Faith, go up to God.'" (And if you don't know a group in your town, you can always call the Abundant Life Prayer Group in the Prayer Tower.)

RIGHT QUESTION   "Medical science is at its highest workable, successful state since it came into being. Polio...diphtheria...smallpox...many more diseases have been virtually wiped out in our country in my lifetime. More diseases are being wiped out all the time. So why don't I get myself under the care of a good physician so I can work with him or her to get God's healing stream of medicine working in my life?" (And if you need a physician at the City of Faith in Tulsa, just phone for an appointment.)

Now those are the kinds of questions you can DO something about.

But back to that first question, "What if Jesus doesn't choose to place His Name directly above my sickness?"

The question *should* be, "Why am I not *putting* the

Name of Jesus above the name of my sickness?"

JESUS has already made it possible for you to do that. The Bible says that God exalted His Name and put it there so that *you* can put it there in *your* own life to meet *your* own situation.

But you have to do it. It's something *you* can do...you CAN do...you *must* do...and something <u>ONLY</u> you can do.

Start asking yourself some other good questions.

<u>Good questions</u>: "Why do I drink alcohol? Don't I know that alcohol is a drug and it will do me more harm than it can ever do me good? Don't I know that alcohol kills brain cells and makes me less than I am? When am I going to quit it forever?"

Put JESUS above the name of "alcohol" in your life.

<u>Good questions</u>: "How much should I weigh to be in the best health? What am I going to do about it? When am I going to start?"

Put JESUS above the name of "fat" in your life.

<u>Good questions</u>: "Why do I smoke? Why do I need this crutch? Why don't I recognize that the faith in me is stronger than my need for cigarettes and that I can be delivered from this habit that is deadly and poisonous? When am I going to quit it forever?"

Put JESUS above the name of "tobacco" in your life.

<u>Good questions</u>: "Why don't I like the church? Why don't I make an appointment with the pastor and sit down and talk? Why don't I give him a chance to help me have a better relationship with God and to get more out of church services? When shall I make an appointment?"

Put JESUS above your "church-hating" or "church-neglecting" attitude.

<u>Good questions</u>: "Why don't I recognize that I have to

give in order to receive? Why don't I become a seed-planter? Why do I expect something for nothing? Why am I stingy and unhappy in my giving? What am I going to do about it? When am I going to get into continual, continuous giving and receiving?"

Put JESUS above your "no-giving" attitude.

The Name of JESUS has become so real, so precious to Oral Roberts that I know every time I lift the Name of Jesus above sickness in my body, my attitude improves. I can see there *is* help. I can see that SOMETHING can be done. I get a new understanding that God is my SOURCE and He's more powerful than anything.

Remember, Philippians 2:10 says:

"At the name of Jesus, *every* knee shall bow."

That's not just a human being's knee. That's every knee of everything in heaven, in earth, and in hell. EVERYTHING must give way to the power of Jesus.

And that's why we...

PRAY IN THE NAME OF JESUS

Do you recall how I told you the preacher prayed for my deliverance from tuberculosis that night in the tent meeting? He prayed:

"Thou foul disease. I command you in the *Name of Jesus* to loose this boy's lungs and life. Come out of him and let him go free!"

That preacher came face-to-face with my disease and prayed in the Name of Jesus. He confronted my disease with the Name of JESUS. He believed without a shadow of a doubt that JESUS was greater than the tuberculosis eating up my lungs and life. He put that belief in motion. He stretched out his hands on me and put his attitude into

135

me.

And then he applied the Name of JESUS to my situation. He helped me believe, too, without any doubt that JESUS was above the name of tuberculosis.

When you pray, pray in the Name of JESUS.

When you pray, see in your mind that the Name of JESUS is greater than the name of the disease or sickness you're dealing with.

When you pray, see the Name of JESUS wiping out the name of the thing that's bothering you.

I've asked you many times now...Are you listening? Do you have a listening heart? If you're listening and you have a listening heart that is working like I believe it is by now, then you can make a quantum leap forward toward being healed and toward getting into healing and health.

You have got to get the Name of JESUS working in your life. You've got to see it for the power it has. And you've got to use it...change your attitude...ask the right questions. YOU have to do it. YOU have to MAKE IT HAPPEN, and I'm here to help you do it.

16

You've got to settle the matter of death once and for all.

I know a lot of people who say, "He wasn't healed. He was a Christian and a good man, and he was even prayed for and went to doctors, but he got sicker and died."

There are several things wrong with that statement. And there are some right things, too.

I want to sort them out for you so you'll never have to be troubled in your mind about death. I want to deal with death in a way that's as honest as you've ever heard.

First, let's talk about what's right in that first statement.

Not all prayers and not all medical help work in the same way for everyone. I myself have prayed for thousands of people in what we called the invalid tent. When we traveled around America in the 1940's and '50's

137

we took two large tents with us because few cities in America had auditoriums that would hold the great audiences that came to our meetings. One of those tents was for people who were too sick to sit through the service. In the invalid tent they could lie down and listen to the service through large speakers.

I always visited the invalid tent after my sermon and prayed personally for each person there. The healing of many began dramatically right there in the tent. But I'm the first person to admit that not every person I've prayed for has gone on to be 100 percent well. Most of them were *helped* in some way, but many didn't recover fully.

You ask, "Why not?"

Well, in many cases, the attitude of the person wasn't a good one. In some cases, the people didn't know how to hold onto the burst of health they did receive. Also, I didn't know then what I know now. I didn't have the experience then that I have now. And in some cases, these people had reached the time – the appointment – for their death.

You say, "What do you mean by appointment?"

The Bible tells us that it is *appointed* for man to die (Hebrews 9:27). You're going to die someday. I'm going to die. There's a time to die. You know that, and I know that.

Our job is to do all we can to make sure we're not too early for our appointment.

You have to understand one thing:

God is God. He is still above medicine or prayer or any other instrument. He may choose to take you to heaven before *you* think it's your time to go. But He is sovereign.

I've been writing to a family whose teenaged daughter has developed a form of cancer. The girl was angry that she had cancer. I wrote her and told her that I had been angry, too, when I first discovered I had tuberculosis. I didn't condemn her for getting angry. That's a good reaction to have. And when the family told me they also were angry, I complimented them for caring so much.

Then I told this young girl that Jesus Christ, through His death and resurrection, is going to heal all of His people. Much of that healing can be done right here in this lifetime. However, the Bible says there is a time to die. I told this girl that there was a chance she might die very soon. She said, "I'm glad you were open enough to talk to me like that." (I find that people want me to be honest and frank with them.)

And then I told her that death is an *appointment*. (I also told her that since we don't know that hour, we would give her our very best. This idea became very helpful and still is as I continue my healing prayers for her.)

Have you ever had an appointment with someone?

I'm sure you have. And you know what happens if you show up early. You just sit around and wait. If you're like Oral Roberts, you get plenty impatient. If you're early for an appointment, you don't get much done. You sit there and watch the clock and fidget and fuss and wonder more and more what will happen when you're finally allowed to go in for your appointment.

Well, that's the same way with some sick people. They get sick and then they just sit around and wait. They quit moving in their lives. They quit working and thinking and planning and believing. They get a sit-down-and-wait attitude. The only thing they're doing with the attitude that's in their hands is twiddling their thumbs.

That's not what God had in mind. Jesus said He came to give us life, and give it more abundantly.

Now God showed me this more plainly in just the past few weeks. I've lived by John 10:10 for many years.

> "The thief cometh not, but for to steal, and to kill, and to destroy: but I am come that they might have life, and that they might have it more abundantly."

139

In fact, "Abundant Life" has been the theme of this ministry for decades and it's the name of our monthly magazine. I believe that Jesus came to give us more than we have ever fully grasped.

But God quoted John 10:10 back to me recently, and in my inner being it's as if I heard it the way that Jesus really said it the first time. I seemed to have heard it with the inflections and the pauses in His voice. I heard it like I'd never heard it before.

He said:

> "For the thief...the devil...cometh not (for any other reason) but to steal...to kill...to destroy."

You see, that's the devil's sole purpose. He doesn't know anything else. And when you feel robbed, cheated, pulled down, reduced, depressed—that's the thief's work. The thief is trying to *rob* you of your life.

> "But...I AM...and I AM come (in the very now of your life...in this moment when the devil comes to destroy you)...I AM come that you might have life...more that you've ever had it...even abundantly."

Throughout the Bible Jesus refers to Himself as I AM. He is All in All. He is the Source. And in this verse He says that He *comes* at the exact moment the devil arrives in your life to steal from, or destroy you. He comes to give you life. He comes to give you life *more* than you've ever had before. He comes to give it to you so that it will be *abundant*...which is beyond all that you expect or need.

You say, "What does that mean to me, Oral Roberts?"

It means that anytime the devil comes into your life before the *exact time* of your appointment with God...anytime he tries to get you into the waiting room early so you just sit around in life and aren't living abundantly, but are being dragged down bit by bit...you are to *fight* him with all you've got. You're to get all the help you can get.

You're to get your attitude squared away and in shape.

You say, "But shouldn't I prepare to die?"

You should. But you do that when you make God the Source of your life and you do that every time you make a choice to do something better about your health and prosperity. You did all that you have to do to prepare to die when you got the Name of JESUS working in your life.

The Bible says:

> "For God so loved the world, that he gave his only begotten Son, that whosoever believeth in Him should not perish, but have everlasting life" (John 3:16).

And it also says in John 6:47:

> "He that believeth on me *hath* everlasting life."

Everlasting life begins when you believe on Jesus – that He died and rose that you might not perish. It STARTS the instant you make Him the Lord of your life – your Savior and Healer.

When you die in the Lord, it is a transition to heaven. The Bible says, "absent from the body and...present with the Lord" (2 Corinthians 5:8). Even before the doctor has signed your death certificate, the King of kings has lifted your soul and taken you into God's presence.

In 1977, my eldest child and firstborn daughter, Rebecca, was killed in a plane crash along with her husband, Marshall, and four other people. I missed her terribly. It was one of the most tragic experiences of my life.

I won't deny that I had feelings of anger, hurt, bitterness, loneliness. But I never felt for a minute that I had seen the last of Rebecca. I know exactly where she and Marshall are. They are with the Lord. I know Rebecca has just changed her address. She and Marshall are alive forevermore in heaven.

Eternity with Christ didn't begin for them on the day

they died. It began the day they gave their hearts to Jesus and knew who they were in Him.

Friend, when you make God the Source of your life and determine deep down inside you to live your life according to God's divine prescription – to put into action what is written in the Bible and to place your confidence in the Name of JESUS which is above all other names – you enter a different time zone. You are no longer awaiting the *end* of your life. You are looking forward to being with the Lord forever. You've got a down-payment on a home in heaven. And as you go along through your life, you're going to have an appointment with God.

Through that appointment He's going to promote you to a new job with a new standard of living. You're going to get the biggest raise you can imagine. You're going to be with *Him*. You'll be continually in His presence and you'll never have to deal with any of the devil's gibes again. You'll be beyond all suffering and all pain. You'll be free of that devil thief once and for all. He can never again try to rob you of anything.

JESUS WILL TAKE THE ONLY CARD THAT THE DEVIL HOLDS

I want you to understand that the devil has only been given one card. He's playing with a deck of one. All of the other cards are held by Jesus.

The card that the devil holds is death. He throws it on the table only once to call the hand of Jesus. He plays it in an instant. And if you have God as the Source of your life, Jesus picks up that card, adds it to His deck, and the devil never has another card that he can play in your life. He's wiped out as far as you are concerned.

That's what Jesus did through His death and resurrection. He made the way for God to get back the only card the devil has ever really had.

When you die and the devil plays his hand, God is

going to take that card; and in the resurrection, He's going to raise you from the dead. The old devil has just lost the game.

And that's the ultimate healing time, my friend— your resurrection from the dead!

It's HEALING TIME for those who have tied their lives to the Name of Jesus. The Name that is above any affliction, trouble, pain, sickness, or *dis*-ease you may have known in life is ultimately...finally...completely...and permanently established as the *only* Name you ever need to know. It completely...ultimately...finally...and permanently wipes out FOREVER any trouble or pain or sickness.

What a time that's going to be!

What an experience is waiting for us!

What a reason to hold up our heads and march confidently and look forward to the day that we have our appointment with God.

And it's also a reason not to rush that appointment. What a charge of energy it gives me to know that God is going to get back the last card that the devil holds. What a great boost to know that God WINS. That gives me the fighting spirit. I want to fight the devil with all I've got until it's God's appointment time for me to be with Him.

You're going to die someday. But until then you're *commanded* to <u>LIVE</u>...and to live more than you are now. You're commanded to get your attitude into your hand and to do something with it to make your *whole* health HAPPEN.

Are you listening?

Are you doing what I've told you to do?

(17)

You've got to take action EACH TIME a crisis hits.

I can almost hear you say to me, "Oral Roberts, it's just great that God healed you of tuberculosis and that you have your attitude working and you're on your way to *whole* health. I guess you've never been in a physical crisis since then."

Well, I'm glad God healed me, too. And I'm glad I found some of those principles to help me get into more and more health all my life. But I've been with my back to the wall more than once since then.

If you're sick now and you get well and on the road to total health, that doesn't make you immune from ever getting some sickness or *dis*-ease in your life again. You're still a human being and in this world of the fall of man, there are still accidents and viruses and bad things that seek to hit at you.

What it *does* mean is that by following God's way you can bounce back quicker, fight harder, and stay on an *upward* track toward health.

I want to share with you something that happened to me.

We opened the City of Faith Medical and Research Center on November 1, 1981. Up to that time we had struggled for four years – against the fiercest kind of opposition ever experienced by us – to get it built and open it so that God's healing streams of prayer and medicine could be merged to help you and others like you.

My partners had stood by me and we had fought the devil and those who opposed us together, side by side. It was a great day when we could say that the City of Faith was *open* and that we could begin to do the work God has called us to do.

Six weeks later the retina suddenly began to slip from my left eye.

I'm not a scientific person – although I have great respect for men and women who are – and the doctors had to explain to me in plain language what was happening. The best way I can describe it is that the back of my eye, which is the part we see with, began to fall away like wallpaper from a wall. And the bottom line was this – if the retina slipped away completely, I'd be blind the rest of my life.

Now I may not have understood all of the explanation, but I understood the outcome very well. I heard it loud and clear when they said there was a possibility I'd be *blind*.

I had to make a decision within one hour to have surgery or not to have it…to have both surgery and prayer working together for me or to limit myself to one or the other. If I didn't make a decision, I would become blind

145

—beginning with my left eye and quite possibly my right.

One noted doctor told me that the reason this was happening might be the stress of the four years we'd just been through. He explained that there are stress points in our physical bodies, just as there are in our cars and houses. When these stress points are pushed too far, something begins to fall apart. That may have been what happened. He said, "The City of Faith has cost you your left eye."

I said to him, "We HAVE the City of Faith open and I *am* going to recover my eye. I'm going to have *both*."

Another doctor chuckled and said, "That's the spirit."

Friend, that is the moment my attitude began to move. I flat out refused to accept the possibility that the devil might steal away my eyes and rob me of my sight. Up until then, I had been sort of numb and uneasy. But suddenly, my attitude came to life.

When you hear a physician tell you what the name is of what you're experiencing as a trouble in your body...or a banker tell you the name of what you're experiencing in your finances...or a spouse tell you the name of what you're experiencing in your marriage...you listen to the explanation and the why's and wherefore's, but you listen *closely* to the OUTCOME of what they're telling you.

I heard the word *"blind."* It was the name of the thing that was about to happen if I didn't take action. You might hear the word *"disabled"* or *"death"* or *"incurable."* You might hear *"bankruptcy"* or *"divorce."*

And at that very point, you take your attitude and you act with it. You say, "No!" You reject that as something the devil wants you to believe so he can reduce you and steal something away from you.

TAKE ACTION WITH YOUR ATTITUDE

DO SOMETHING to keep that thing from happening. Deep down inside, I had some good things going for me. I believe God is the Source of my life. I believe He is the Source of my health. I believed I was at the right place at the right time. I believed that prayer and medicine should work together.

And I took action.

I told the retina specialist, "I will enter into an agreement with you and cooperate with you 100 percent in the surgery you need to do to repair my eye. Get whatever you need. I will also cooperate 100 percent with the power of prayer. My decision is made."

I'll always believe that was the turning point. It was the single-most decisive thing in saving my eyesight. I'll tell you something. When it comes to your health, there's no time to be indecisive.

And when I had my attitude right and I had taken action with it, things started happening.

Nothing was really happening until then. As soon as I had made my decision, the doctors and associates around me scattered.

One went to call my darling wife Evelyn. One went to call the Abundant Life Prayer Group in Tulsa to get the best of prayer moving in my direction. Some went to arrange for a surgical team that could be available to operate in just a few hours. (That was no easy task. You see, it was Friday night and I was in Los Angeles. That is the night of the week they call the "killing night" in L.A. It's the night when there are the most violent crimes in that city. Every hospital is overflowing and the doctors and nurses are working at full steam. It would not be easy to get a surgical team arranged for an early Saturday morning surgery.)

And they all left me. They had bandaged my eyes and walked away.

They left me sitting alone in that examining chair. And I tell you, it was one of the loneliest times I have ever known.

Later, I was told I had only sat there for less than 30

147

minutes. But it felt like much longer because I was doing business with God.

As I sat there, I sensed that God was closer to me than my breath and that we were going to work together in my recovery from this eye condition. I didn't know He was going to speak to my heart. I only knew that I was in this predicament without my choice...that I had made a firm decision to move forward in prayer and medicine...that my attitude was grounded firmly in God as my Source.

And then...

Deep within me I heard that same voice I've heard so many times since I first heard it in the back seat of the car Elmer borrowed to drive me to the healing service. (The Word of God—the Bible—is always my guide through the power of the Holy Spirit. But I've come to recognize the voice of God.) I heard from within me the Lord saying, "You will *not* go blind. You *will* recover your sight."

Almost as soon as I heard those words, I heard the negative words of the devil trying to jam God's signals to me.

I knew it was the devil because of what he was saying to me: "I've been trying to get you for years. I have thought I had you but I didn't. But now I've got you where I want you and I'm going to get you. I'll stop your ministry. Tonight is the end."

I knew that was a possibility. If I went blind it would be almost impossible to do the work that I do on television and in writing and speaking and praying for the sick. I also knew that it would be a victory for the devil that would cause people to have less faith in God.

But I also knew it was a *lie*. And I immediately resisted the devil and told him to leave me. I was no more aware that he was in the room.

Then the Lord said in the words that I've longed to hear since I was 17. He said, "Son, I am going to show you My-self. I'm going to show you My glory. After that, I'm going to show you who you really are...to Me and to millions of others."

As soon as I heard those words I remembered something that had happened in 1947 just before I began my ministry of healing. Over a period of 30 days, I had read the Gospels consecutively—Matthew, Mark, Luke, John and the book of Acts through on my knees. As I did this, I would see Jesus rise up out of the pages of God's Word. I'd feel Him seize my heart with the feelings He had about lost and suffering humanity.

At the end of that period, I may not have seen Jesus with my physical eyes, but believe me, I saw Him from the Word as real as I will ever see Him. He became so real to me that I knew Him and how He talked and walked and moved about in His ministry.

But this was something different.

I said, "What do You mean, Lord? What do You mean, You're going to show me Yourself? How could I ever be able to see You?"

He said, "Just accept what I am telling you...that I will show you Myself. After that, I will show you My glory. Then who you really are."

GOD SHOWED ME ABOUT ATTITUDE

The Lord moved on quickly to <u>DO</u> what He said He was going to do. The first thing He showed me about Himself came almost immediately.

He showed me that attitude is everything. I could have given in to the injury or ailment striking my eye and cried, "Why did this happen to me? What did I do to deserve this?"

I could have fallen apart, blaming God for what had happened. I could have thrown life into a frenzy.

On the other hand, I could have stood tall inside believing the Bible and believing that sickness is an oppression of the devil, and I could take hold of my attitude. I could learn that the way God puts our attitude to work in us is more powerful than any negative thing that can attack us.

The Lord showed me that He had given us our attitudes and that we were to do something with them. The choice is ours. And I decided to put my attitude on God's side.

When the doctors came back into the room, I had become alive in my spirit—almost electric in my attitude. The main specialist noticed it and said, "Say, if I didn't know about the retina in your eye, I would think something good has already happened to you."

I said, "Doctor, something good *is* happening to me. The whole thing is going to turn out *good.*"

He said, "Great! Now that's the kind of patient I like to have. I've had friends who told me you were like this. But it's really a powerful encouragement to me to know that you really are that way."

(And it will be an encouragement to *your* doctor, too, when you talk to him with that kind of attitude working full steam.)

We're starting to see that same attitude in our partners who come to the City of Faith. The doctors tell me the "hope level" of the City of Faith patients appears to be up about 20 percent. Scores of our doctors have told me that the greatest pleasure of their lives is in practicing medicine and healing prayers together with patients who believe that both together are going to work in their behalf.

I can feel this attitude every time I walk through the City of Faith. It emanates from the people. And it flows back from me to them.

Then that eye specialist asked, "What do you want me to call you?"

I said, "Well, Mama named me Oral."

"Fine, I'll call you Oral." And then he said, "Oral, I'm going to work." He put his hand on my knee and said,

150

"You talk to the Man upstairs while I and my team go to work surgically."

I said, "There's one thing you can count on. I am a *part* of this healing process."

I was eager to get on with the surgery. You see, I was making a prime-time television special there. I would have given anything in the world to have my own eye doctors and surgeons in the City of Faith do the surgery. But there was no time. I was just blessed that I had two of my doctors with me in Los Angeles and that they had directed me to the best eye doctor in the world who was available at the moment. And I was doubly blessed that this man had the *spirit* of the City of Faith in him. He didn't divide the natural and the supernatural. He appreciated what we are doing at the City of Faith, merging God's healing streams of medicine and prayer. He was comfortable with his own medical skills, and he was equally comfortable with the power of prayer.

Then they took me to the hospital. I discovered that more than half of the nurses and other workers there were partners of my ministry. As often as possible they would lean over and say, "I'm a partner and I'm praying for you."

Never mind that I was in a strange hospital hundreds of miles from home. I knew that God had placed His natural and supernatural best at my disposal. I knew my attitude was under my control. I knew I could use my attitude to actually inspire the people around me to be more effective in their medical skills. By the time I was prepared for surgery, I simply couldn't wait for it to start.

I was in surgery for three hours, and another three or four hours in the recovery room.

I could hear the voices of the nurses and doctors and my associates, but I couldn't see them. They had left the bandages over both eyes and they told me they would remain there for three days. They were for my protection...but because of them, it was as if I were blind. I couldn't see a thing.

Dr. James Winslow, who helped me build the City of Faith, was with me before and after the surgery. He had been the one to lead me to the car, drive me to the hospital, put me in the elevator, and stay with me until the surgical team took over. He told me later, "Oral, I've always known you are an obedient man. And since you've been my patient twice, I know you are a good patient. But it nearly killed me when I saw you unable to see and I had to tell you to raise your feet, turn left, turn right, avoid hitting this wall, get in this elevator, and so forth."

I said, "Jim, those three days and nights – those hours when I couldn't see and I lived in total darkness – that time took me back to 1947 when Jesus spoke to my heart and said, 'I'm going to let you see people as I see them and hear them as I hear them.'"

The Lord had done that for me. Night after night I would awaken and see the people as the Lord saw them – sick and suffering in some way. The Lord gave me a feeling for the sick that I've never lost. I came to love the sick. And to love them so much that I was willing to touch them no matter what disease or sickness they had. I've touched more than a million people in the world and prayed for their healing.

I concluded, "During those days of darkness, Jim, I felt a new love for sick people. And I got a special feeling for the blind. It's a feeling that will drive me to find better answers from God."

There were moments of panic during that darkness, too. I want to tell you about them because you might experience the same thing sometime.

You see, not only was I in a medical emergency, I was in a *ministry* emergency. I had signed a contract to make a prime-time television special and some weekly half-hour programs, and we were to begin taping the programs just five days after the retina began to slip away from my eye.

The contract was for a fairly large sum of money and there was no way to cancel it without losing the money and going off the air for an entire month. That would have been the first time I had not been on television since 1954.

Panic hit me in the pit of my stomach, and once I vomited. That was a combination, of course, of the anesthetic and the stress that was trying to fasten itself on me like an octopus. The devil was again breathing down my neck and repeating what he had said before, "I've got you now. Your ministry will stop."

Again I said to him, "No!"

I grabbed that attitude of mine every possible moment and kept saying in my heart, "God, You are my Source. I've planted my seeds of faith. I'm expecting a miracle to bring me through this and back on the television stage in a few days." And believe me, I meant it.

I was at the point of great need. I was looking to the Name of JESUS to overcome and wipe out this fear. I was recalling as many scriptures as I could from the Bible. (And it's amazing how the Holy Spirit will help you remember scriptures you have read and studied to help you when you are in trouble.)

And, friend, I tell you today that God met me at the point of my need.

The patches came off in three days. And two days later I was in front of those television cameras. If you saw those programs you know how I shared about my surgery and told it like it was. I was wobbly and my eye didn't look very good...but I was there. And I was preaching the best I could. I was planting seeds of my faith. I was making my sermons my Point of Contact to get even more healing.

Somewhere during those hours of surgery, a burst of healing had come into my body. I held onto it with all I had. I wasn't about to let go.

And in that attitude, the Lord spoke to me some of the most powerful things I've ever heard. I'm going to share them with you in the next chapter so you can get these things working better in *your* life and attitude.

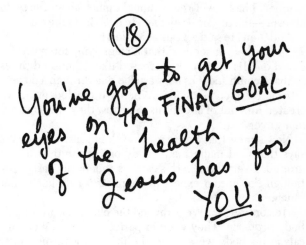

18

You've got to get your eyes on the FINAL GOAL of the health Jesus has for YOU.

As I regained more and more of my health after my eye surgery, the Lord began to speak to me again.

He began to show me Himself in a way that had never crossed my mind.

I began to see Jesus.

Now I saw Him through my spiritual perception in my inner being. I didn't see Him with my eyes because they were covered with bandages. I saw Him with my inner vision.

He took me back to His birth and let me see how He was conceived in the Virgin Mary by the Holy Spirit. He was completely God in His Spirit. But His body was grown in Mary's body. It was made up of the substance of her body, for His birth was physical in the same way that you and I have had a physical birth.

I knew that was true but it hadn't occurred to me in that manner. I had never really thought much about the *body* of Jesus—the physical self that He lived in on the earth.

And then He said, "Look at My left eye."

As I looked, it seemed that a magnifying force was focused on His eye and it increased like a thousand times so that I could see it as if I were looking through a powerful microscope. He said, "When we created man, we created him out of chemicals. See how they are arranged in my eye?"

Now I knew that we are made of chemicals. Genesis 2:7 says that God made man's body out of the dust of the ground. Everything in this earth is chemically based. Although I'm not an expert in chemistry, I do know that much.

He continued, "We arranged the chemicals in Adam's body *properly*. They were in perfect order. The chemicals in his body were perfectly lined up with his spirit. And he *dis*-arranged those chemicals by his disobedience and the Fall in the Garden of Eden. All of his offspring were plunged into some form of *dis*-arrangement in their chemical make-up. The perfect arrangement of the mind and spirit was shaken up."

And then He said, "But I was born of the Virgin Mary, with the same chemicals that all human beings have. The chemicals in My body were again put into perfect arrangement. One of My highest purposes in coming to earth was to make it possible for those chemicals to be *re*-arranged in every person's being...to put the chemicals back in the right order. And that's why I'm showing you My eye in magnified form."

This was way beyond my ability to understand and yet I seemed to understand it. Jesus knew that I was wondering what all of this had to do with me, Oral Roberts.

156

He said, "What I had the surgeon doing in the surgery room was *re*-arranging the chemicals in your eye."

I said, "O Lord, this is all beyond me."

He said, "No, it isn't. Just stop and think a moment. God is the Creator...and you and all other human beings are His creation, including everything in this earth. No chemical the Father put in this earth in the beginning has ever been lost. Everything is still here in some form for the health of yourself and others. But...it must be *re*-arranged so that it is more like the way it was first put together in the Garden of Eden. In the resurrection all of it will come together again in a perfect way."

And then He went on to say, "I want to tell you further about My Incarnation."

You may ask, "Oral Roberts, what's the *Incarnation*?"

That's a word we use to say that God became man. It is a mystery that defies our minds unless we accept it in our spirit and by faith.

Before Jesus came, it was difficult to understand God, because no person had ever seen Him. When He came in the form of Jesus, we had a better way of understanding Him. Jesus was both God and man at the same time—totally God and totally man. When we read about Jesus in the Bible, we can begin to see what God is like, to understand Him better, and to come to love Him and obey Him with all our hearts. We can also begin to understand the possibility of what *we* might be like as human beings.

The Incarnation also has to do with the Cross. Jesus had to go to the Cross—to be crucified and die so that He could be a sacrifice for all humanity. Each of us now has a way to be forgiven of our past sins and to become new creatures in Jesus Christ (2 Corinthians 5:17). Everlasting power was set in motion so we could be completely restored back to God.

The way was also paved for Jesus to return to earth again some day. And a new heaven and a new earth would replace everything we know today.

I knew all of that about the Incarnation, and I believed it. I've shared it with you. But apparently there was something I had missed that God wanted me to know…and to share with you.

Jesus shifted my inner vision to the Cross and I was able to see the Crucifixion—not with my physical eyes but with a vision that was far more penetrating. I saw the jeering crowds, the hateful crucifiers, the Roman soldiers who did the actual nailing of Jesus to the Cross, and the whole of humanity. He let me experience it in my spirit.

And He said to me, "You have thought you understood the Incarnation and the Cross. You have understood much of it, but you have missed what I'm going to show you now.

"Far beyond the giving of My life on the Cross to provide forgiveness of sins and to let people come into everlasting life, I came to AFFIRM human beings. You have known that the Cross is the price that the Father paid to get back a lost and suffering mankind for Himself. You have been told that man is worthwhile because God paid such a high price. But there's even more to it than that.

"As I hung on the Cross, enduring things that no human being will ever fully know, it was done so I could say to every man, woman, and child:

"God affirms you as a human being— made physically with chemicals—and a living soul—made in God's image and likeness. The attitude of the Father toward you has been completely reestablished through my death and resurrection.

"Provision has been made to re-arrange everything that has been dis-arranged. We—the Father, Son, and Holy Spirit— see you as a person who is going to be re-created into My likeness so that the chemicals in your body can be *re*-arranged. Many of them are in *dis*-arrangement. Whatever is out of harmony in your life can now be put back into harmony again. Beginning here on earth in the now and through death and beyond—you will be completely restored through my resurrection if you believe and receive My life."

The scene suddenly changed and I began to understand the sheer miracle of chemicals for the natural order of the earth. They are forever connected and interconnected in a supernatural arrangement that God designed and put into operation on earth.

I saw that every chemical needed to bring us to perfection was someplace and in something on the earth.

I saw how the chemicals could be *re*-arranged to bring us back into the perfection that God had made in the beginning. I could experience a little of the glory of God as I saw the design and the plan that He had made.

Those were powerful words to me when Jesus said:

> "I died to *affirm* mankind and to restore him."

You say, "What does *affirm* mean, Oral Roberts?"
It means to make *the most positive statement possible*.

And Jesus was saying to me that those who believe in Him are going to be made perfect. God hasn't given up on you. He still sees you as His highest creation.

We can now have a spiritual relationship with God like the one Jesus has. We can now have a *body* like the one Jesus had—with the chemicals perfectly arranged. And we can get more and more of that spiritual relationship while we're here on the earth. We can get more and more of that body while we're here on the earth.

Can you see what that means to you for your healing

and health?

Are you listening?

Do you have a listening heart?

It means that *whole* health is having the same kind of health that Jesus had...has...and will always have.

It means that Jesus wants you to be whole. He has made provision for it to happen. It's going to happen. And it can START happening now.

It means that it is not only possible but AFFIRMED that you *will* have whole health and prosperity.

You *are* going to know the same kind of perfection in the resurrection that Adam and Eve knew before they sinned. The order has already been placed. The wheels have already been set in motion. Jesus' death on the Cross was the beginning of it all.

And we have to get in step with His plan so it can start happening in our lives today...now...this very minute.

When we really get it inside us that there was once a perfect arrangement, and that God has made a way for it to be perfect again—we're going to run after health. We're going to really go after it in a new way.

When you get it deep inside you that God has a perfect arrangement for your body—for all the chemicals inside it and outside it...

When you get it deep inside you that God has a perfect arrangement for your spirit and your mind and your body to come together as a *whole*...

You're going to *run* after health, the kind that is whole-person health.

You're going to want it more than anything else.

You're going to want God to *re*-arrange more and more and more of you so that you're far along on your way to health long before your appointment for death and your resurrection.

You're going to begin to see that God's plan for your health is stronger than any plan that the devil has to keep

160

you from getting it.

You'll begin to see that prayer is one of the divine ways God uses to get that *re*-arrangement going.

You'll begin to see how doctors and others can be used to *re*-arrange the chemicals in your body in better order.

You'll begin to see how right eating and right sleeping and right exercise and right climate can all come together to *re*-arrange the chemicals in your body so that they are more like what God planned for you, and is working to recreate in you.

You'll begin to see how a right attitude can get you on the road to a right relationship with God.

You'll begin to see that everything you do to get your attitude is a seed that you are planting...and that the harvest can be your physical, emotional, spiritual, financial *whole* self in the Lord.

You'll get a glimpse of the glory that God has in store for you. You...YOU...*YOU*!

And when you do, my friend, it's going to get you so excited that you will desire to have health in a greater way than before. You'll go after it as God intended you should...and can.

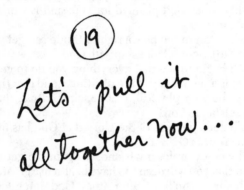

(19)

Let's pull it all together now...

I'm going to lay it all out as a complete prescription for you...just like a doctor gives you a prescription, except this may be the best prescription you've ever had or will ever have.

I'm going to try to pull all of these things together so you can see them as a whole. And the reason I'm doing this is so you can turn again and again to these pages and they can remind you that you have to MAKE SOMETHING HAPPEN for your better health and prosperity.

I expect these pages to be worn out from your reading them...week after week...and on and on.

I *command* you, in Jesus' Name, to do these things.

There are twelve parts to this prescription. Read them

slowly and let them sink in, one by one, and then as a whole.

ORAL ROBERTS' PRESCRIPTION FOR YOUR HEALTH

1. *Get God into your life in a way that He's never been there before.* Accept Him as a good God and reject any lie you ever hear again that God has in any way caused sickness or poverty or broken relationships. Deal God into your life. Make Him your *Source*.

2. *Get your attitude going in the direction of living instead of dying.* Start thinking about *more* instead of less. God wants you to have His riches—of health, of love, of prosperity. Take charge of your attitude.

3. *Put your attitude into action.* DO SOMETHING. Make some decisions and get going.

> Get hold of some people who know how to pray. Make them your friends and partners. See your physician. Get to know him or her. List some specific things that you can DO. Get your attitude in your hand and put it to work.

4. *Plant.* Take your life—your money, your time, your love, your good attitude—and *invest* it in God's fertile soil. Keep planting seeds of faith continually and continuously.

5. *Make your seed-planting a Point of Contact for each point of need in your life.* For every need, plant a seed. Plant a seed to get over the hurdles in your way to whole health—whole physical health, whole relationships, whole minds and spirits, whole finances and the material goods you must have. Use seed-planting as a Point of Contact to turn your faith loose and say, "Faith, go up to God."

163

6. *Grab hold of each burst of healing you receive.* Accept it. Believe it's real and keep on going. Get more health. Don't stop.

7. *Place the Name of JESUS above the name of anything that causes you to have dis-ease.* See in your mind the Name of JESUS washing away the name of any sickness or *dis*-ease you have.

8. *Run TOWARD the goal of whole health that God has for you.* God has a perfect health for you...a perfect arrangement for your mind, spirit, and body...a perfect relationship with Himself. What you don't get here on earth, He has waiting for you at the time of your resurrection. But get all that you can HERE and NOW...even today.

9. *Decide today that you are going to carry out this prescription.* You *can* carry it out. *ONLY* you can carry it out.

10. *Write me about it.* As you carry out this prescription, tell me the bad and the good. Tell me when you're up and when you're down. Tell me like it is. Then I can write you back and help you again and again.

Now I've put one page here for you to tear out. Carry it with you or put it on your desk. When you find yourself down and sick or troubled, get this out and read it. Ask yourself these questions. Get back into this book and find the answers.

I NEED HEALING... I CAN DO SOMETHING TO MAKE IT HAPPEN FOR ME!

1. Have I made God the Source of my entire life, including my healing?

2. Do I have hold of my attitude and am I causing it to move in the right direction?

3. Am I doing anything to MAKE THINGS HAPPEN for my better health and prosperity? Have I done all I can do to put my attitude into action?

4. Am I planting seeds so God can grow them and multiply them back to me? Am I expecting a harvest?

5. Am I using a Point of Contact REGULARLY so that my faith is CONTINUALLY and CONTINUOUSLY going up to God?

6. Am I holding onto the burst of health that I've already experienced?

7. Have I placed the Name of JESUS above the name of the thing that is troubling me?

Tear out this page and keep it handy.

8. Am I really GOING AFTER the health and prosperity that God has planned for me?

9. Have I really decided that I'm going to DO this...and do it TODAY...right NOW?

10. Am I working with Oral Roberts to have a Blessing-Pact relationship with God?

**I CAN LIVE BY
THE 3 KEYS OF
SEED—FAITH**

**Make God your Source
(Philippians 4:19)**

**Give, and it shall be given to you
(Luke 6:38)**

Expect a miracle (Mark 11:24)

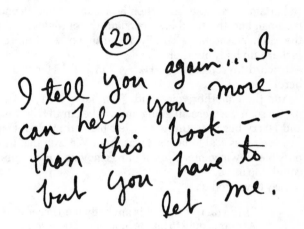

(20)

I tell you again... I can help you more than this book — — but you have to let me.

Are you going to let me help you?
Have you been listening?
Are you developing a listening heart?

When I was a boy I played on an American Legion baseball team. We had a pitcher named Harry Bracken who went on to be big league when he grew up.

One day we were out on the field and we were losing. We were up against a great team, and we were believing that they were better than we were. Harry was pitching and the ball just wouldn't go across the plate. We were losing and we felt it.

Now our coach had taught us to "talk it up" out in the field...to get a little "hey, batter; hey, batter" chatter

167

going. But we weren't talking it up right then. We were standing around like a bunch of zombies. It was q-u-i-e-t out there.

Suddenly Harry stopped. He looked over at Oral Roberts on first base. And then he looked at the second baseman and the third baseman and the outfielders and the catcher. And he yelled, "Is there anybody out there? Is there anybody out there?"

I heard myself saying, "Harry, I'm here! Harry, I'm here!"

And then another voice said, "I'm here, Harry!" And pretty soon we were all going and we began to talk it up and Harry began to throw that left-handed pitch of his. I can see it as real today as it was then. We *won* that impossible-to-win game. We got things moving and nothing could stop us.

I say to you today:

> "Are you out there? Is anybody out there? Are you going to let me help you? Have you been listening? Are you going to *DO* something to *MAKE THINGS START TO HAPPEN* for your health and prosperity?"

Now I want to say a word about START. Every long journey in this world begins with a START. You never go anywhere unless you start. It would be nice if we could take giant leaps and get instant miracles that are over in a split second. It would be nice if we could have everything all at once. But that isn't the way it is. What you *can* do is START toward those miracles. That's something *you* can do...you can *DO*...and ONLY you can do.

You see, I believe God has given us the opportunity to stand with each other. It's no accident in God's plan that you have this book in your hand. It's no accident that you have read it all the way through. God has given us the opportunity to love each other, to write to each other, to believe with each other, to join together.

The Bible says in Galatians 6:2:

> "Bear ye one another's burdens, and so fulfill the law of Christ".

And James 5:16 says:

> "Pray one for another, that ye may be healed."

And in Matthew 18:19 Jesus said:

> "If two of you shall agree on earth as *touching* any thing that they shall ask, *it shall be done* for them of my Father which is in heaven."

That's powerful.

I can't stand with you if you won't let me.

I can't touch anything and agree with you unless you let me.

I can't write you a letter unless you write me first.

I can't speak to you in the Name of Jesus if you aren't listening.

I want to see you well...

I want to see you moving into health and prosperity...

I want to see you become a *whole* person in every area of your life.

But I can't help you if you won't let me.

Are you listening?

Do you have a listening heart?

Then GET UP...

GET GOING...

GET MOVING...

CARRY OUT GOD'S PRESCRIPTION FOR YOUR LIFE.

And do it *TODAY*...NOW...THIS VERY *HOUR*.

Healing Scriptures I Use Often and Offer to You for Quick and Regular Reference...

Beloved, I wish above all things that thou mayest prosper and be in health, even as thy soul prospereth.—3 John 2

For I say, through the grace given unto me, to every man that is among you, not to think of himself more highly than he ought to think; but to think soberly, according as God hath dealt to every man the measure of faith.—Romans 12:3

The thief cometh not, but for to steal, and to kill, and to destroy: I am come that they might have life, and that they might have it more abundantly.—John 10:10

How God anointed Jesus of Nazareth with the Holy Ghost and with power: who went about doing good, and healing all that were oppressed of the devil; for God was with him.—Acts 10:38

And Jesus answering said unto them, They that are whole need not a physician: but they that are sick.—Luke 5:31

But they understood not this saying, and it was hid from them, that they perceived it not: and they feared to ask him of that saying. Then there arose a reasoning among them, which of them should be greatest. And Jesus, perceiving the thought of their heart, took a child, and set him by him, and said unto them, Whosoever shall receive this child in my name receiveth me: and whosoever shall receive me receiveth him that sent me: for he that is least among you all, the same shall be great.—Luke 9:45-48

And he said unto him, Thou hast answered right: this do, and thou shalt live.—Luke 10:28

Behold, I give unto you power to tread on serpents and scorpions, and over all the power of the enemy: and nothing shall by any means hurt you. Notwithstanding in this rejoice not, that the spirits are subject unto you; but rather rejoice, because your names are written in heaven. In that hour Jesus rejoiced in spirit, and said, I thank thee, O Father, Lord of heaven and earth, that thou hast hid these things from the wise and prudent, and hast revealed them unto babes: even so, Father; for so it seemed good in thy sight.—Luke 10:19-21

And I say unto you, Ask, and it shall be given you; seek, and ye shall find; knock, and it shall be opened unto you. For every one that asketh receiveth; and he that seeketh findeth; and to him that knocketh it shall be opened. If a son shall ask bread of any of you that is a father, will he give him a stone? or if he ask a fish, will he for a fish give him a serpent? Or if he shall ask an egg, will he offer him a scorpion? If ye then, being evil, know how to give good gifts unto your children: how much more shall your heavenly Father give the Holy Spirit to them that ask him?—Luke 11:9-13

And he asked his father, How long is it ago since this came unto him? And he said, Of a child. And ofttimes it hath cast him into the fire, and into the waters, to destroy him: but if thou canst do any thing, have compassion on us, and help us. Jesus said unto him, If thou canst believe, all things are possible to him that believeth. And straightway the father of the child cried out, and said with tears, Lord, I believe; help thou mine unbelief.—Mark 9:21-24

And Jesus answered and said unto him, What wilt

thou that I should do unto thee? The blind man said unto him, Lord, that I might receive my sight. And Jesus said unto him, Go thy way; thy faith hath made thee whole. And immediately he received his sight, and followed Jesus in the way.—Mark 10:51,52

But Jesus turned him about, and when he saw her, he said, Daughter, be of good comfort; thy faith hath made thee whole. And the woman was made whole from that hour.—Matthew 9:22

And Jesus said unto them, Because of your unbelief: for verily I say unto you, If ye have faith as a grain of mustard seed, ye shall say unto this mountain, Remove hence to yonder place; and it shall remove; and nothing shall be impossible unto you.—Matthew 17:20

When Jesus saw him lie, and knew that he had been now a long time in that case, he saith unto him, Wilt thou be made whole? The impotent man answered him, Sir, I have no man, when the water is troubled, to put me into the pool: but while I am coming, another steppeth down before me. Jesus saith unto him, Rise, take up thy bed, and walk. And immediately the man was made whole, and took up his bed, and walked: and on the same day was the sabbath.—John 5:6-9

Jesus saith unto her, Said I not unto thee, that, if thou wouldest believe, thou shouldest see the glory of God?—John 11:40

Jesus saith unto him, I am the way, the truth, and the life: no man cometh unto the Father, but by me.—John 14:6

Even so faith, if it hath not works, is dead, being alone.—James 2:17

Confess your faults one to another, and pray one for

another, that ye may be healed. The effectual fervent prayer of a righteous man availeth much.—James 5:16

Is any thing too hard for the Lord? At the time appointed I will return unto thee, according to the time of life, and Sarah shall have a son.—Genesis 18:14

I Can Give You Additional Information That Will Help You.

Will You Let Me?

☐ Oral Roberts, please send me FREE information on how I can get started on a Blessing-Pact with God. Send me information right away so I can begin to get a harvest-bearing field planted in my life.

☐ Oral Roberts, please tell me more about your Bible with your commentary in the back. Tell me how I can have one for myself.

☐ Oral Roberts, please mail me, free and post-paid, a copy of your book, MIRACLES OF SEED-FAITH.

Name _____

196

Address _____

City _____ State _____ ZIP _____

Tear out this page and mail to:
Oral Roberts, Tulsa, OK. 74171

Here I am with Mama and Papa in 1965. When I was a
17-year-old boy dying with tuberculosis, Mama and
Papa called in the best doctors they knew. At the same
time they started praying and calling people of our
church to pray. They taught me many things about
having a good attitude toward God and that He was the
Source of all healing power.

My son Richard and I stand shoulder-to-shoulder in this ministry of God's Word. And with us in every way are my darling wife Evelyn (left) and Richard's wife Lindsay (right).